Workplace Politics

A Practical Guide
for Making Your Experience at Work
More Positive, Productive and Pleasant

Bruce Grossman, J.D.

To order additional copies of this book, contact:
Xlibris Corporation
1-888-795-4274
www.Xlibris.com
Orders@Xlibris.com
19275

Contents

PART FOUR: CONTENDING WITH VARIOUS PERSONALITIES AT WORK

PART FIVE: MOVING ON

DEDICATION

To my wife, Claudia, without whose unconditional love and support this book could not have been written; to my parents, Dena and Bernie, who, whether they knew it or not, taught me to have the confidence to follow my dreams; and particularly to my Dad, Bernie, who proudly supported me through this project, but unfortunately did not get to see it completed.

INTRODUCTION

The Purpose of this Book and How It Can Help You

INTRODUCTION

The Purpose of this Book and How It Can Help You

The focus of this book is on creating a better understanding of people's working relationships and identifying strategies for how to more effectively and productively deal with the individuals with whom you may work. It is *not* a book about how to climb the proverbial "corporate ladder." Rather, the purpose of the book is to assist people in making their work experiences more positive, productive and pleasant.

Although the book is entitled *"Workplace" Politics*, it is really intended to apply to all organizational situations in which people relate to or interact with other people during the course of an average day. Those situations might include work situations for pay; situations or organizations in which people work as volunteers; private, nonprofit and governmental organization situations; and organizations from every region. Everyone in every type of organization, small or large, manager or non-manager, should be able to identify with and benefit from at least some of the examples referenced or strategies explored in this book.

My perspective is that of an attorney who has been practicing in the employment law field for over twenty years. I have provided extensive advice to individual employees and managers in organizations and have been confronted with many negative work-related situations. I have seen workplace conflicts develop; have attempted to defuse those conflicts before they escalate; and have seen the effects of those conflicts when they cannot be defused.

Through the course of these experiences, I have observed many people at a variety of levels and in a variety of types of organizations who are unhappy with their work situations and would like to make those situations more positive, but are at a loss as to how to accomplish that. I have spent countless hours over the years counseling friends, colleagues and clients about "political" issues at their workplaces; about how to get along with others at work; and about how to make things better for them at work. As a result, it occurred to me that perhaps there are many people in all walks of work life who also might be able to benefit from such counseling and/or the development of political strategies at work to make their situations more positive and productive. This book has been written to try to provide some insight and assistance in those areas with those types of individuals in mind.

* * *

What I have tried to accomplish here is to anticipate some of the more common workplace scenarios and offer some strategies for how to turn those problem areas around. All efforts have been made to structure the book in as user friendly a format as possible. In most Chapters, relevant examples are presented and practical suggestions for how to handle those situations are offered.

The examples used throughout the book are composites of real-life situations. Some even contain caricatures of the various personality types described. The examples are used solely for the purpose of illustrating the points and strategies raised. Although *based* on real-life situations, the examples have specifically been set up as "hybrids" and with the use of caricature personalities so as *not* to be recognizable with any specific, real-life situations that may have actually occurred, in the interest of protecting the privacy of the individuals involved.*

Hopefully, everyone can personally identify with the various personalities involved and/or relate to the factual situations described in this book. I am hopeful that people will read the examples and be able to say to themselves: "Yes. That happened to me (or someone whom I know or observed at work)." It is my view that, if people can *relate* to the situations or individuals described, they will be able to better help themselves in attempting to resolve those issues when they *do* arise in their own real-life work situations.

* * *

The *types* of scenarios presented and the *types* of personalities described are present in *every* workplace in one form or another, regardless of the particular industry in which you work, or the particular job that you may hold. Further, the suggested strategies explored throughout the book apply equally across the board to all types of work environments and all types of jobs as well.**

* * *

---

*   *In a further effort to keep the characters referenced in the book not identifiable with real-life persons, and in an effort to keep them gender-mixed, the characters used in the examples also arbitrarily alternate between being female and male, with no relationship necessarily to real-life people on which the examples might be based in some cases.*

**   *Please note that this book is not an answer to everyone's work-related problems. There may be some specific work-related issues or situations which cannot be resolved at all; which require specific counsel or guidance from your own personal lawyer, therapist, or clergy person; which may require the filing of a formal complaint with your employer or a governmental agency; and/or which may necessitate that you seek employment elsewhere. In addition, this book is also not intended to provide specific legal advice for any specific work-related problem. Individual legal problems require in-depth attention and analysis to determine the appropriate strategies and solutions specifically tailored to address those problems, given the specific personalities, circumstances, and workplace dynamics involved. If you need assistance with a specific legal issue that arises in your workplace, you will need to consult with your own personal attorney.*

It is my sincere hope that there is something in this book for everyone in every kind of workplace or organization. My ultimate goal is to provide information and suggestions which are practical; user friendly; enjoyable to work through; and helpful in assisting you to hopefully resolve some of your workplace issues.

PART ONE

Getting Started

CHAPTER 1

Preview of Coming Attractions: The "3P" Approach

This book offers practical suggestions for how to deal with common issues that arise from time to time at the workplace. The goal is to assist people in making their work experiences more *positive*, *productive* and *pleasant*.

Part One of this book provides some useful background information regarding how to "get started" in your quest for developing strategies for making your work experience more positive. This Chapter provides a short summary of the overall subject areas and strategies which are addressed throughout the book. Chapter 2 provides an analysis of exactly what is meant by the term "Workplace Politics." Chapter 3 explores ways to figure out exactly what it is that you *want* from your job.

In Part Two, political strategies common to all workplace situations are explored. These strategies have universal application, regardless of the type of job you have or the type of organization you work for.

For example, all of the following can have an impact on how

positive your work experience can be: (1) developing the right attitude toward your work; (2) knowing when to pick your battles and which battles to pick; (3) understanding that your actions create "impressions" on others and that the "image" you project, whether you like it or not, affects how others will respond to you; (4) understanding exactly what it is that you want out of your job, organization, or career; (5) seeking positive reinforcement at your job; and, most fundamentally, (6) competently performing the work that you are employed to perform.

These concepts are developed in Chapters 4, 5 and 6 of Part Two. The overall purpose of Part Two is to assist you in understanding that you have the ability to control, or at least shape, others' opinions of you at work which, in turn, could assist you in making your overall work experience more positive and productive.

Further, in order to truly develop a positive, enjoyable work experience for yourself, it is also critical to understand how some of the common individual employment *relationships* work. Part Three is directed at strategies designed to maximize your ability to get along and work well with individuals with whom you interact directly at your workplace, such as co-workers, supervisors, subordinates, partners, and owners of organizations. Included in Part Three are discussions of common underlying motivations of managers and non-managers; and the relationships that various management level persons may have with each other.

With respect to the dynamics between managers and non-managers in particular, it is not uncommon for busy managers to lose sight of what is important to, or what motivates, their staff members, or to be unaware of the particular sensibilities of those staff members. On the flip side of that coin, it is also common for non-managers not to be privy to or fully understand all of the issues that motivate their managers to act or treat them in a certain way. Clearly, one key to maximizing the positives of your work experience is to develop an understanding of what individuals with whom you work think, and attempt to motivate or respond to them accordingly. Chapters 7 and 8 of Part Three specifically explore those particular issues in some depth.

In addition, Chapter 9 of Part Three is aimed at developing strategies for dealing with family members, as well as individuals whom you may need to deal with on a regular basis at work but who do not actually work within your physical environment. Included in Chapter 9, for example, is a discussion of "family politics." Many of us are prone to bring our work home with us physically, mentally and/or emotionally. How our family members react to our working at home or bringing the "baggage" from the work day home with us can, of course, dramatically impact on our overall outlook toward our jobs.

Chapter 9 also explores relationships with other "third parties" who can impact on your workplace situation, such as customers and clients. Understanding the dynamics of these relationships might assist you in making your work experience more positive as well.

Part Four of the book identifies certain personality types that you may be likely to face at work and offers suggestions for how to work best with those individuals. Obviously, it is not possible to list every conceivable personality type that one might encounter in the workplace. However, some of the more common ones, such as the "Bully," the "Screamer," the "Charming Backstabber," the "Ruthless" individual, the "Control Freak," and the "Nitpicker," are discussed respectively in Chapters 10 through 14 of Part Four.

We have all encountered these types of personalities in various forms and to varying degrees at one point or another at work. The discussions of these personalities include caricature descriptions of the personality types, with suggestions for how to work effectively with them.

Finally, to the extent that, despite your best efforts, you have reached a point at which your job situation is simply no longer workable or salvageable for you, Part Five (Chapter 15) provides some suggested strategies regarding "political" issues which could arise in looking for a new job. Included in Part Five are some tips on how to handle and make use of former supervisors as references; networking; and, when appropriate, using recruiters to assist you in your job search.

CHAPTER 2

What Is "Workplace Politics"?

This Chapter is intended to educate you on the importance of acknowledging the existence of "politics" at the workplace and the need for political strategies to assist you in getting what you want from work.

Definition of "Workplace Politics"

Everyone has a separate relationship of *some* kind with each of the other persons with whom they work. "Workplace politics" involves the development of (1) an understanding of those relationships and of how people interact with each other at work; and (2) strategies for managing each relationship effectively, dealing with other people at work, and getting what you want from them.

"Politics" Exists in Every Organization

Every workplace, small or large, has politics and political issues in one form or another. Everyone wants *something* from his or her job. Everyone has a goal or agenda of *some* kind, even if that goal is simply to do a good job. (Goals are addressed in more detail in the next Chapter.) In order to achieve their goals at the workplace, individuals typically will have to interface with other people; need assistance from some of those people; and have to contend at least to some degree with other people's goals and agendas. As a result, dealing with "political" issues at work is simply unavoidable.

(If you are ever on a job interview with a prospective employer and you are told by members of that organization that "there are no politics here" or that "we are above such mundane things as 'politics' in this organization," be *very wary*. There is simply no such thing as an organization that has *no* politics or is "above the political fray." People who tell you that their organizations do not have any "politics" to contend with either are naive or perhaps are not being completely truthful with themselves or with you.)

No one likes to *think* that there *are* politics in his or her organization. Nor do people like to think that they need to develop and employ "political strategies" in order to succeed at work or to make their workplace situations more positive and productive. Such a concept seems to run counter to the common notion of justice and fair play that, if you work hard and do your job well, you will be judged on your merits and will be appropriately rewarded for your efforts.

Further, many people tend to think of the concept of "workplace politics" as a *negative* thing and that workplace political "strategies" are unnecessary and perhaps even counterproductive. Those same people refuse to believe that their ability to succeed at work (however they define success) can be *influenced*, even to the slightest degree, by such an intangible thing as "workplace politics."

However, the following two concepts simply need to be accepted as true in order to successfully develop and implement strategies for making your work environment more positive. First, "politics" *does* exist in all workplaces. Second, political strategies commonly *need* to be employed in order to maximize your chances of making your work experience more positive; helping yourself at work; and, ultimately, getting what you want from your job.

Types of Common Workplace "Political" Issues

Jobs, promotions, assignments, reporting relationships and careers can and often do turn on "political" issues at work, rather than on the pure merits of an individual's work performance.

Consider the following. Have you ever been passed over for a promotion because it was given instead to someone whom you are absolutely convinced does not perform at your competence level? If the person is truly not performing at your competence level, how did he or she get the promotion? Have you ever wondered why (or how) your supervisor could possibly be convinced that your co-worker is a star, based solely on the fact that the co-worker continues to *tell* the supervisor that he or she *is* a star? Have you ever wondered why you are not getting sufficient credit for the fine work that you perform? Have you made your supervisor *aware* of the work that you have done or of the positive results that you have achieved?

*   *   *

All of these issues involve workplace politics to one degree or another. Some forms of workplace politics are simply more palatable than others. The larger the organization and the more personalities that are involved, the more complex the political issues within that organization can be. However, any organization that employs more than one person has workplace political issues in *some* form.

In fact, even organizations with only one person have political issues. That individual may, for example, still have to interact with his or her clients or customers and sometimes will have to pacify dissatisfied clients or customers. Developing techniques for dealing with those individuals is a form of workplace politics.

The Use of "Political" Strategies at Work

Workplace political strategies are commonly *necessary* to help most people achieve what they want at work. Of course, everyone must assess his or her own work situation and the personalities he or she works with to determine which strategies should be employed and how to employ them in the context of his or her particular job.

One caution about the use of "political" strategies at work should be noted. Whatever strategies you choose to employ in the context of your work situation should be applied discreetly and with subtlety where possible. As noted earlier in this Chapter, most people are uncomfortable with the thought that "politics" even plays a part in their organization. In addition, and perhaps more significantly, some people might view a workplace political strategy, rightly or wrongly, as a form of manipulation, and no one wants to believe that he or she is capable of being "manipulated." Note that, to the extent that people are made aware of the existence of a "political strategy," they are likely to become *more* defensive, refusing to believe that they could possibly *allow* themselves to fall "victim" to such a strategy.

Ultimately, your goal is or should be to get what you want from your workplace situation. Be mindful of the fact that you will be less likely to get what you want at work if your co-workers feel defensive or manipulated, or if they believe that they are a "pawn" in some "strategy."

CHAPTER 3

Setting Goals - Figuring Out What You Want from Your Job

The very first step in developing political strategies for making your work environment more positive is to figure out what you want from your job, both in the short run and in the long run. Everyone wants *something* from their job.

The purpose of this Chapter is to help you identify what it is that *you* want and what you believe will make *your* working environment more positive, productive and pleasant for *you*. Only after you successfully identify what makes you happy in your job; what makes you feel positive about your job; and/or what assists you in being productive in your job, will most of the strategies discussed later in this book make sense or be useful to you.

Identifying Your True Workplace Goals

The ultimate question here, and one that you should ask yourself, think about, and try to answer as carefully and truthfully as possible is, "Exactly what is it that I want from my job, my organization and/or my career?" Understand that everyone will answer this ultimate question differently because people have different ideas about what their workplace goals are or should be.

Consider the following examples as illustrations of how some people identify their various goals. First, there is Sam, a production manager at a company that employs several hundred people. Sam's job is very "nine to five." He makes enough money from this job, along with his wife's income, to support his family, which includes two children.

The job is not very challenging for him. His overall performance is consistently evaluated as "average," although in some categories he might be slightly below average. He does not want to be challenged at work and rarely takes initiative to get things done without specifically being directed to do so. His lack of initiative is sometimes frustrating for his supervisors, which causes some friction at times between Sam and his supervisors. He also from time to time has trouble getting along with some of his co-workers.

Sam views his job as "just a job" which is necessary to pay the bills, not a stepping stone in a "career." In fact, Sam does not regard himself as having a "career;" nor does he particularly want one.

Sam's goals with respect to this job are fairly straightforward. He wants to work productively during the time that he is actually at work; avoid working long weekdays or any weekend hours; and perform his job at a basic competence level so that he is not in danger of losing it. He is not likely to be very stimulated at work or to get promoted (unless his goals change), but he is completely comfortable with that. In short, his goal is simply to maintain the status quo.

*   *   *

Next, there is Donna. Her one and only priority in life is to see as much of the world as she possibly can. She stays in one place just long enough to earn enough money to travel again.

Her lifestyle is simple. She does not accumulate much wealth and, when she does travel, she does so quite economically.

She is also a sculptor. When she travels, she collects artifacts and other usable materials that she then uses to make small pieces of jewelry, as well as larger sculpted pieces, which she then sells. To make ends meet, she also takes on odd jobs both while traveling or when at home. Her goal is to succeed at the jobs she holds for just long enough to accumulate the "pocket money" she needs to move on and/or work on her sculpting.

* * *

Next, we come to Charlie, who is an attorney. He has worked for one law firm continually for his entire career. He has proven himself to be extremely competent at his job and his been quite successful in continually achieving positive results for the firm's clients.

Although he works very hard, he is quite efficient with his time. Every day, he works from eight to six-thirty and eats lunch at his desk. He makes himself available to put in whatever hours are necessary to perform his job competently, but working nights and weekends is not a regular occurrence for him.

Although he is cordial with co-workers at work, he tries to mind his own business and do his work. He rarely socializes with co-workers either during the day or after work.

Charlie lives modestly; does not take extravagant vacations in the years when he even takes vacations; and saves and invests as much each year as he possibly can. His priority is to build a large "nest egg" for himself, so that he can retire by age 45. He has understood from the beginning that, if he worked hard and impressed his bosses, his salary would increase each year, which it has, and that he would be made a partner in the firm after five years, which he was. He also understands that, as a partner, his income will increase dramatically each year, which it also has.

Charlie has kept his goal of retiring at age 45 in mind from the time he first started working for the law firm at age 25.

* * *

Finally, there is Susan. Susan is a senior executive at a Fortune 500 company. She is charming, charismatic and very hard working. She performs her job extremely competently and has been continually rewarded for her efforts. She has worked for the same company for nearly 20 years.

Susan has been promoted eight times, each time to increasingly powerful, stimulating positions which have provided progressively increased responsibilities; increasingly large staffs of people to manage; and, ultimately, greater input into corporate decision-making and the overall corporate vision for its future growth.

At each stage of her career, Susan's goal has been to work in her current position for two years and then seek a promotion to the next managerial level. Her long-term goal is to ultimately be promoted to the very top of the corporate management structure.

Questions to Ask Yourself

In an effort to assist *you* in answering *your* ultimate question of what *you* truly want from *your* job, the following samples of background questions should be considered. (Understand that these are not necessarily the *only* questions to ask, but are some basic ones which can help you get started in figuring out what you want from your job.) Try to think about these questions as you wrestle with the identification of your workplace goals.

Remember, there are no right or wrong answers to these questions. What is important is that you be honest with yourself in identifying what really is important to you, so that appropriate, workable strategies can be developed which truly meet your particular workplace needs and goals.

Questions Relating to Personal Goals

Are you looking for a certain level of personal job satisfaction, regardless of the level of power, influence, or responsibility you have or the amount of money you make? Are you looking to get along better with the people with whom you work? Are you looking just to be left alone to do your job? Are you looking to get credit for doing a good job? Are you looking to help others achieve their goals? Is your goal to create a more positive overall working environment, not just for yourself, but for others as well? Is your goal to be more assertive and not allow yourself to be taken advantage of? Are you looking to create a situation in which you have control over your own fate? Is your goal just to keep your job?

Questions Relating to Family and Relaxation Goals

Is attention to family issues more of a priority than work? How high a priority is preserving relaxation time and taking vacations?

Questions Relating to Time-Oriented Goals

How long do you want to stay in your existing job; in your existing home; in your existing town? Where do you see yourself in six months, one year, five years, ten years? Do you see yourself in this job? Do you see yourself in *any* job?

Questions Relating to Longer Term Goals

Is your primary goal to accumulate as much wealth as you possibly can? To climb the proverbial corporate ladder? To get a particular promotion or a series of promotions? Do you want progressively increased responsibilities, power and influence at your job? Is your goal to manage a staff or department of people? To one day run the organization that you presently work for? To one day run *any* organization?

*   *   *

The purpose of this Chapter has been to emphasize the importance of figuring out exactly what you want from your job; to demonstrate how goal identification can work in practice; and to illustrate how to set goals for yourself. Working through some of the questions in raised in this Chapter will hopefully assist you in figuring those things out as they apply to your particular workplace situation.

Further, now that you have a basic understanding of how goals fit into the overall workplace puzzle, you are ready to explore core political strategies which can help you to achieve those goals.

PART TWO

Basic Workplace Truths

CHAPTER 4

Doing the Work

The Core of Workplace Politics: Doing Your Job

Consider Anthony's situation. He has a great attitude about his job. He is always willing to pitch in. He has successfully created an image for himself as a team player. He rarely turns down work. He works very efficiently and always gets his work done ahead of scheduled deadlines. He is always looking for new projects. His overall work experience is quite positive, in no small part because he **does his job** and **does it well**.

* * *

As the above example illustrates, a universal workplace approach that everyone should adopt in their efforts to make their work situation more positive, productive and pleasant is to make sure that they "do the work." There is simply no substitute for actually doing the work that you have been charged to do. Above all else, **do your job**.

All of the other political strategies explored throughout this book are incidental to, and should be used in conjunction with, the primary workplace strategy of "doing the work." Whether or not you choose to employ various political strategies, those strategies will typically have little effect on your ability to make your work environment more positive if you do not make your best efforts to perform the work that you have been hired or assigned to perform.

"Doing the work" is certainly not a guarantee that you will have a work experience which is positive; that you will be judged solely on your merits; or that you will achieve your goals or attain the kinds of successes that you want at work. However, failure to "do the work" will commonly be an assurance that you will *not* have a positive and productive work experience or be treated with the level of respect at work that you would like.

What It Means to "Do the Work."

"Doing the work" can mean a number of different things, depending on the type of job you have. In every job context, however, "doing the work" means (1) working hard; (2) putting in the time, energy, hours, and effort necessary to effectively do your job; (3) trying to perform at your highest possible level of competency at all times; and (4) working as efficiently and productively as you can. "Doing the work" means **doing your best**.

"Doing the work" means doing the work *well*; impressing the people who need to be impressed; and achieving positive results, whether those results involve winning, increased sales figures, making money for your organization, or satisfying the demands of clients, customers, board members, or others who may be judging your work. "Doing the work" also means (1) demonstrating a willingness to work long hours, early mornings, late nights, and/or weekends, if and when necessary; and (2) doing whatever is necessary, within reasonable job-related parameters and legal boundaries, to maximize the likelihood of achieving the results that you need to achieve.

"Doing the work" also involves creating **perceptions** that you work hard; are a team player; and are doing your best. Most supervisors will give employees some slack if they believe that the employees are trying their hardest to do their best work. On the other hand, employers are typically far less forgiving of employees whom they perceive to be *capable* of performing their jobs at a certain competence level, but are unwilling to or fail to actually perform at that level for whatever reason. (More about creating positive perceptions about yourself is addressed in Chapter 6.)

"Doing the work" means having a positive attitude about your job and not being too contentious or disagreeable. No one wants to work with someone who is constantly complaining. The last thing that you want is to develop a reputation as a complainer or, worse yet, someone who is unwilling to do his or her job.

Finally, "doing the work" involves doing whatever you are asked to do, again within reasonable job-related parameters and legal boundaries, without complaint or other indication that you are unhappy or unwilling to perform those tasks. It means not complaining about the type of work that you are doing; the volume of your workload; or particular assignments that you have been given. (You should note that, if you are unhappy over a period of time with the work assignments that you are getting, you *will* need to schedule some time with your supervisor to discuss those issues. In those instances, be prepared to discuss possible alternative work assignments and/or have suggestions for creative solutions to the concerns you raise ready for your supervisor's consideration.)

*　　*　　*

Remember, it is your boss' organization (or at least they are closer to control or ownership of the organization than you are).

They ultimately get to decide how the work assignments get distributed and how the work should be done. Try to "do the work" in the manner that your boss envisions that you will do it and/or instructs you *to* do it.

Why Should I "Do My Work" When Others Are Not Doing Theirs?

Perceptions of Others' Work Habits Are Often Inaccurate

A common misconception about some individuals at work who seem to be enjoying more successes than others is that they somehow manage to achieve their successes without actually "doing their work." However, although people sometimes may have *perceptions* that others are succeeding in their jobs without "doing the work," those perceptions are commonly inaccurate.

Consider the following example. Melvin is a CPA. He has worked out a schedule under which he only needs to physically come in to work on Tuesdays and Thursdays. Although he has part-time status, he does do some work from home on other days. He is well-liked by most of his supervisors and his clients are very satisfied with his work.

Some co-workers resent him, however. Many of the co-workers are not aware that he performs work while at home. Others simply do not think that he works very hard. There are also perceptions among his co-workers that (1) he is paid proportionally more for his part-time work than some employees are paid for their full-time work; and (2) he manages to avoid getting "called on the carpet" for things for which others get chastised, perhaps by virtue of the fact that the other employees are simply present at work more of the time.

To Melvin's credit, he understands the need for and implements certain political strategies at work to maximize the likelihood that he will get what he wants. He successfully communicates all of his accomplishments to the influential people with whom he works; and he has created an image of being a team player, a hard worker, and a winner. However, his successes at work are based on the facts that he *does* do the work; *does* work hard; sometimes *does* do work while at home or out of the office; and *does* get good results. Melvin also has a positive attitude; does not complain; does try not to turn down assignments unless absolutely necessary; and, even when he *does* occasionally turn down assignments, he *does* make sure that his allies are aware of the (usually work-related) reasons for having to turn them down.

*   *   *

A common misconception about Melvin (and others like him) is that he manages to always to come out "smelling like a rose" without actually doing his work. It is true that what commonly distinguishes individuals like Melvin is that they typically *do* have highly developed political skills and commonly *do* know how to build a positive image of themselves in their organizations. However, what co-workers are often unaware of is that these individuals also *do* take care of necessary business on the "home front" by, in fact, "doing their work."

Try not to be mistakenly lulled into believing that individuals who happen to have charming personalities and/or who happen to have employed certain political strategies or created positive images of themselves at work are getting away with *not* "doing the work." The truth is that, while there is the very occasional employee who can manage to succeed at work based on image and personality alone, particularly in the short run, people at work are typically judged, at least to some degree, by their actual work performance over the long run.

In addition, try not to make assumptions about the work that co-workers may or may not be doing generally. As is evidenced by Melvin's example, you may not always be privy to all of the necessary information about those co-workers and may be presuming things that either are not true or may be based on speculation, or incomplete or inaccurate information. (Avoiding jumping to erroneous conclusions about your co-workers is also likely to make you less resentful of them, which, in turn, could assist you in making your work experience more positive.)

Preparation Is Everything

It is also important to try not to be mistakenly lulled into believing that individuals who make their job tasks look easy or who seem to have more natural talents, gifts, or skills than others in their abilities to perform their jobs well are somehow getting away with not "doing *their* work."

Consider the example of the public speaker who makes her speech seem so effortless and natural that she creates an aura that she is not working very hard. What most people see, however, is the end result of a tremendous amount of preparation.

Take Julia, for example. She prepares fresh outlines for her speeches every time she gives one, even if she has given speeches on the same subject many times before. She consistently does fresh research for updates to her speech materials. In addition, she reviews her speech outlines over and over again prior to each presentation so that they are basically committed to memory. This helps make the speech seem seamless.

In her speeches, she can typically answer any question presented in any sequence and cover the response to that question in detail, whether or not that material has been covered in the speech up to that point. She can reorganize her entire presentation while in the midst of it if the audience shows an interest in going in another direction. She presents an air of confidence in her expertise and makes it look easy.

What the audience does not see, however, is the extensive preparation that is commonly involved in making such a presentation appear so smooth, spontaneous, and free flowing. All that the audience sees is the flawless end result.

Whether the audience is aware of it or not, however, Julia certainly "does the work" in order to achieve her end results.

She, like most people, needs to prepare extensively for her successes at work. The mere fact that her audience and/or her co-workers do not *see* her working hard does not mean that she is *not*, in fact, working hard.

*   *   *

Consider the additional example of gifted athletes. The public perception of many of these individuals is that they succeed primarily because of their natural talents and that they do not work very hard to achieve their successes. In most cases, this is simply not true. Although many of these individuals do have tremendous talents to start with, they often would not achieve nearly the level of success that they do without actually putting in the time to "do their jobs." Most of these individuals work incredibly hard at developing their skills and their crafts; train hard to keep well-conditioned; practice hard; and/or study films of potential opponents.

*   *   *

As the examples illustrate, it is important to understand that the extent of the work that individuals who make their job tasks look easy do may not be readily perceptible to co-workers. In most instances, there *is*, and there needs to be, a substantial amount of *preparatory* work which is done behind the scenes without which successful results could not be achieved.

For the overwhelming majority of us, preparation is everything. Most of us need to prepare extensively in order to succeed in our jobs.

In addition, the examples of Julia and the gifted athletes also illustrate two basic truths that people should remember about perceptions about co-workers and the extent to which they are "doing the work." The first is that virtually no one can continue to succeed at work over a prolonged period of time, no matter how talented they are, without getting down into the trenches, doing the work, working hard, and doing the work well. The second is that those with less natural talent who do the work and do the work well will typically tend to enjoy more successes and positive experiences at work over the long run than those who have the natural talents but are less tenacious about actually doing the work.

"Doing the Work" and Staying Out of the Political Fray

In football, sometimes the best offense is a good defense. Similarly, in the workplace, sometimes the best political strategy is simply to do the work and stay out of the political fray. Sometimes, "doing the work" may even be the *only* political strategy that you need to employ or should employ.

Consider the following example. Monica and Samantha are managers who work for the same organization. They have shared responsibilities for supervising a group of employees.

Although they need to get along to some degree for the greater good of their departments, and/or the greater good of their organization, sometimes they have their own political agendas and/or do not like, trust, or respect each other. In those cases, one or both of them might be looking to gather support from their staff members in their efforts to usurp the other's authority or to embarrass the other.

* * *

The best strategy for those working with Monica and Samantha (or other managers like them) might simply be to "do the work." Stay out of the line of fire and steer clear of battles, particularly when they are not yours. Try to remain neutral and helpful to both sides. Avoid taking sides where possible. Show everyone an equally positive attitude. Try not to betray the confidences given to you from either side and try to avoid jumping on either's bandwagon or presenting one camp's point of view when in the other camp (particularly when it will not be perceived as being constructive).

"Doing the work" successfully (and staying out of the political fray) under those circumstances might be the *only* strategy which engenders the confidence of both managers, while not alienating either, and keeps you out of the line of fire.

*   *   *

In sum, there is a reason why it is called "work." No one is *entitled* to their job. Having a job involves "working." The reason that you get paid is to "do the work." All employers have the right to expect, and can even demand, that, in exchange for getting paid, you will in fact ***do your job.***

CHAPTER 5

Common Workplace Strategies: The Bare Essentials

Two basic premises underlying this entire book are that getting what you want will enhance your ability to make your work experience more positive; and *failing* to get what you want is likely to make your overall work experience less positive. In Chapter 3, some suggestions for assisting you in figuring out exactly what you want from your job were discussed. One reason for proceeding with that exercise was that, in order to actually *get* what you want, you first need to *know* what you want. Once you *know* what you want, you then need to figure out how to *get* it.

Sometimes, developing and implementing certain "political strategies" can assist you in that effort. This Chapter explores some basic "political strategies" which are generally applicable to all workplace contexts and are designed to assist you in getting what you want.

Always Keep Your Own "Big Picture" in Mind

One core "political strategy" is to maintain perspective on what your true goals are and to keep your own "big picture" in mind at all times. What this means is that you should try to (1) never lose sight of what your priorities are and what you want; (2) never lose sight of how to get what you want; (3) not get caught up in *other people's* goals and agendas; and (4) avoid engaging in conduct which does not *assist* you in getting what you want.

Before engaging in any conduct at work which could impact on getting what you want or making your overall workplace experience more positive, and in an effort to keep perspective on your own "big picture," ask yourself the following questions: (1) Exactly what is it that I want out of this situation? and (2) How does the conduct that I am about to engage in help me get there? (Bear in mind that, if your contemplated conduct does *not* assist you in getting what you ultimately want, perhaps it should not be engaged in at all or should be modified so that it *does*.)

Consider the following example. Laura is an employee who has worked for her company for four years. She was passed over for a promotion.

She never discussed the issues of whether she *wanted* to be promoted and, if so, when she *expected* to be promoted, with management. In fact, management was not even aware that she was *interested* in being promoted.

Laura also never evaluated for herself whether she in fact even *wanted* the promotion. Even after the promotion decision was made, she was still unclear about whether she would have wanted it. Nevertheless, she was upset that she did not get the promotion and would have liked to at least have been *asked*.

After the promotion announcement was made, Laura decided to speak with members of senior management directly. However, because she remained unsure about whether she really even wanted to *be* promoted, she had formulated no concrete plan with respect to what she hoped to accomplish by speaking with the management team. She simply desired to vent her anger and tell management why she believed that it had made a poor decision.

Nor did she want to hear about her own performance deficiencies.

What she wanted was to use this "opportunity" as a vehicle to air a number of grievances about her employer which were not necessarily even related to the specific promotion decision.

* * *

How should Laura have handled this situation? First, what she should have done was figure out exactly what she wanted from the situation, both in the short run and in the long run; and then come up with a game plan for how to get it. It would have been advisable for Laura not to speak with her supervisor or any member of senior management in her organization until she understood exactly what she wanted to get out of those conversations.

Specifically, it might have been useful for her to evaluate whether she really *wanted* the promotion at all and/or whether she would want a similar promotion if and when it became available in the future. The tone and direction of her conversations with management would then need to be shaped appropriately, based on her answers to those questions.

If she determined in hindsight that she *did* ultimately want to be promoted, perhaps the conversations with management would be better directed at developing an understanding of why she did not *get* the promotion, so that she could improve herself for next time. In that instance, she would need to be prepared to have a frank discussion about her own performance deficiencies. A discussion in which she simply vented her anger in that context would likely be counterproductive.

By contrast, if she determined in hindsight that she *did not* want the promotion, either now or in the future, it might be appropriate for her to reevaluate the necessity of raising this issue at all. Rather, it might have been useful in that context to analyze in advance exactly what she hoped to gain from talking to management about it. If not handled correctly, such discussions might make management defensive and alienate Laura to some degree from some members of the management team.

Further, if Laura's goal was truly to bring issues unrelated to the promotion to the attention of management, perhaps it would be more productive to raise those issues at a time when the promotion issue was not being discussed. Raising those issues at the *same* time could link them in the minds of the senior managers, which would not necessarily best assist Laura in getting what she wanted with respect to those issues.

Finally, if Laura's goal was merely to inform management that she was displeased with the *manner* in which the promotion was handled, perhaps it would not have been the best strategy for her to *attack* the decision-makers. Rather, a better strategy under those circumstances might have been to have a calm, frank discussion with the manager with whom she has the closest personal relationship, during which she could explain *why* the *manner* in which she was informed about this decision was humiliating to her on a personal level. The goal of such a conversation might be to assist management in how it would handle such matters in the future.

*   *   *

In short, how Laura (and others like her) should handle this situation depends entirely on exactly what she (and others like her) desire to get out of it. As a general rule, employees are usually better served by not diving head first into a situation without asking themselves what it is that they want from the situation and whether the behavior that they are about to engage in is likely to help them get it.

*   *   *

Consider the additional example of Jane and Cindy. They are both physicians. They went to medical school together and did their residencies together. Both specialized in internal medicine.

During medical school and their residencies, both expressed

interest in working in smaller communities where they could establish general practices in which they could develop longer term, personal relationships with their patients and have what they believed to be more personally gratifying lifestyles and practices. The primary goal of both individuals was to remain dedicated to helping patients in need in any way that they could.

However, when their residencies were completed, both Jane and Cindy were substantially in debt and had student loans to pay off. For that reason, both moved to larger cities and began working for established medical groups in those cities. Their separate practices quickly proved to be high volume, high pressure, highly visible, and very lucrative.

When she started working in private practice, Jane adopted what she referred to as her "five-year plan." Her goal was to pay off her debts within five years; save a substantial sum of money during that time; and then move to a smaller community where she would establish her smaller, less pressured, more patient-oriented general practice. She understood that her smaller community practice would be less lucrative for her, but she always remained mindful of who she was, and what her ultimate goals and priorities were.

Cindy, on the other hand, entered her big-city medical practice without creating a plan for herself and without setting goals for how to ultimately set up her small community general practice. Instead, she got caught up in all of the money that she was making. She paid off her debts but, rather than save the money she earned, she purchased a house which was more than she could afford.

As her income increased, so did the cost of her lifestyle. She purchased a second home, which was quite large, but barely affordable for her. In fact, despite her large income, she struggled to make ends meet.

Cindy surrounded herself in her practice with wealthy physicians who owned large homes and whose primary priorities, unlike Cindy's, were to accumulate large amounts of personal wealth. She also insulated herself by socializing only with neighbors, friends, and colleagues who had similar priorities and goals to those physicians with whom she worked. Although it was not her preference to do so, she felt compelled to simply "keep up with the Joneses."

In addition, her relationship with her spouse and her family deteriorated dramatically, though commitment to family matters had been a high priority of hers as well.

She commonly did not take or return calls from troubled family members and failed to attend to their problems with the necessary patience and concentration, because she was "too busy." In fact, she became quite notorious for not returning calls from friends or family for weeks or months at a time, and regularly postponed family vacations or had to reschedule landmark family events because of work-related issues.

*   *   *

The Jane/Cindy scenario illustrates just how important it is over the long run to keep your own objectives in mind and not get caught up in other people's goals and agendas. Somewhere along the line, Cindy's goals and priorities became sublimated to the goal of simply acquiring more and more wealth.

She got caught up in other people's goals and agendas. She was not happy with her job, her career or the life and lifestyle that she had created for herself. Rather, she felt trapped by her lifestyle and had reached a point where she was not enjoying her medical practice at all. She lost sight of who she was and what she wanted, and failed to maintain perspective on what was ultimately important to her.

The key to not letting that happen is to always be mindful of who you are; what matters most to you; and what you want out of your job. It is easy to get caught up in work-related pressures and making money, for example, particularly when everyone around you considers those issues to be of the highest priority. It is difficult to remind yourself that, although you will do your best, those things may not be as personally important to you as other issues. However, being mindful of priorities and keeping them straight could help Cindy and others like her avoid making choices which make them unhappy and/or make their work experiences considerably more negative.

* * *

The bottom line here is to make sure that you stay focused on what it is that you want and how to get there. Remember, the keys to succeeding in getting what you want are to (1) develop strategies with your goals, perspectives, priorities, and your own "big picture" clearly in mind; and (2) make every effort to avoid engaging in conduct which does not *help* you in getting what you ultimately want, either in the short run or in the long run.

Be Patient

Sometimes, in order to get what you want from your job or from a workplace situation, you need to be patient. We all have instincts from time to time when facing certain workplace situations to react to them immediately. However, very few issues that arise in the workplace truly *are* urgent and/or truly *need* to be resolved or acted upon immediately.

Be aware that sometimes you need to address issues one at a time; one step at a time; and/or as they arise. Try not to project all possible negative consequences of a given situation. Doing so may turn out to be premature and unnecessarily stressful.

Generally, it is usually a good idea to take the pressure off yourself of needing to resolve every workplace problem immediately. Allow yourself to relax into your work situation; learn the ropes; and plan your strategies. Doing so is likely to reduce your stress levels; assist you in getting what you want; and make your job more enjoyable.

Slow and Steady Wins the Race

Sometimes, things can take days, weeks, months or even years to develop and you may need to just let them develop in their own time. In addition, some things manage to work themselves out on their own without ever having to address them at all.

Try to develop strategies slowly over time and force yourself to avoid impulses to change direction or strategies simply because you are too impatient to see them through. Take your time. Talk to colleagues. Come up with strategies that make sense for you and are consistent with both your short-term and your long-term goals. Then patiently wait for those strategies to unfold properly and in their own time.

Consider the following example. Ruth was initially a mid-level manager at a mid-sized company. She was promoted several times over a number of years until she finally became a Vice President. In that capacity, she had substantial hiring, firing, and recruiting responsibilities, among many others. She had become a major player in the organization; was a member of the senior management team; and had commanded the respect of co-workers and other senior managers alike.

From the time that she first started working for the company, however, until significantly after she was promoted into her Vice President position, she remained in a very small, cramped office. Numerous times during her tenure at the company she had been offered larger offices which, to some degree, could have better accommodated her increasing workload. She continually turned them down because, at each turn, there were other individuals at her level or higher whom she believed were (or who perceived themselves as) more appropriate choices for the better offices offered. Her goal in her rise through the corporate ranks was to be a power player in the organization and not step on too many toes or make too many enemies in the process.

During all of this time, Ruth was building her power base. She tried not to make waves. She worked hard and had an extremely positive attitude. She did everything that was asked of her. She was being patient and biding her time.

Eventually, a very large corner office opened up when one of the other senior executives retired. This time, she accepted the company's offer to move her into that office. By the time she finally moved into her corner office, no one close to her level at the company (above or below) had any legitimate, credible objections to her taking it, which is exactly what she had been waiting for.

*　　*　　*

Ruth always wanted a big corner office. She chose not to settle for anything less and to wait for a time when a corner office opened up and no one could possibly object to her taking it over. She was always mindful of her goals; had a strategy in place for achieving those goals; and was extraordinarily patient in allowing that strategy the necessary time to unfold.

Opportunities Inevitably Present Themselves

Another important component of being patient at the workplace involves waiting for opportunities to present themselves. Opportunities to resolve workplace issues almost always *do* present themselves eventually. You may not think at a particularly anxious moment that such an opportunity will *ever* arise, but it is at that moment in particular that you need to be most cognizant of stepping back and patiently waiting for the opportunity *to* arise.

Consider the following example. Karen has a complaint about Ned, one of her supervisors. Her instinct is to go to Dean, another supervisor at the same level as Ned. She wants to confront the problem immediately but, after thinking it through, decides that she will wait for an opportunity to present itself with Dean. She works with Dean a great deal; frequently spends time speaking with him about a variety of workplace issues; and, overall, has a positive working relationship with him.

Karen looks for the right opportunity to lodge the complaint about Ned with Dean, in a context where the complaint might be taken seriously and when Dean might actually be inclined to do something about it. She knows from working with Dean over the years that he is extremely busy and largely unapproachable in the mornings and early afternoons. She looks for an opportunity to talk with Dean at the end of a work day when he is calmer, more relaxed, and more approachable.

Late one night at work, Karen finds herself alone with Dean, discussing a variety of work-related subjects. During this conversation, Dean actually confides in Karen that he is having some frustrations of his own with Ned.

Karen now senses that the moment has arrived. After waiting patiently over several weeks, the opportunity has finally presented itself for Karen to make her complaint to Dean about Ned, which she does. Dean is receptive; listens carefully to Karen's concerns; and indicates that he will attempt to resolve the issue on Karen's behalf either directly with Ned or with his colleagues.

*   *   *

The reason that this issue can successfully be resolved for Karen at this moment is that she developed a strategy and patiently waited for the opportune moment to maximize the likelihood of getting what she wanted from the situation. Had she rushed into such a conversation with Dean, she might have unnaturally forced the issue and would have been far less likely to have the issue addressed and/or resolved in the manner that she wanted.

*   *   *

As the Karen/Ned/Dean example makes clear, opportunities to address critical issues inevitably present themselves at some point. The key to this strategy is to *recognize* the opportunity when it *does* arise and be prepared to *act* at that moment.

Try to avoid "marching" or "storming" into your supervisor's office with what you perceive to be an urgent problem, however.

Understand that you are far more likely to get what you want from a given situation or job if you appear to be reasonable and credible, as opposed to angered, hysterical, over-reactive, nervous or panicked. Sometimes, it takes time, patience and/or a strategy that involves thinking before acting to appear reasonable and credible, rather than panicked or angered.

It is typically a better strategy to try to wait for the moment when the issue arises naturally, instead of forcing the issue and requiring co-workers to deal with it before it is ready to be dealt with. Remember, if you force the issue, you might be less likely to ultimately get what you want.

* * *

In short, try not to be in such a hurry to resolve your workplace issues immediately. Understand that sometimes things have a way of working themselves out. Have the patience in most instances to think before acting; to develop a meaningful strategy; and to wait for the opportunities to resolve those issues to present themselves. They invariably will, and you may be more likely in that context to get what you want than you would have been had you not waited.

Pick Your Battles

Another instinct that many of us have at the workplace is to fight back when we feel challenged or backed into a corner. However, not every issue is worth fighting about and not every battle should be fought. In the interests of (1) getting along with co-workers and managers; and (2) maximizing your chances of actually *getting* what you want, it is important to carefully pick your battles at work.

Consider the following example. Victoria is a self-righteous employee. She fights whenever she perceives there to be an unfairness done to her or to someone else with whom she works.

She fights to "right" every proverbial "wrong." There is no workplace injustice which is too small for her to take on.

She fights about her parking space being too far away from her work station. She fights about the vending machine in the company lounge not having diet sodas. She constantly complains about the temperature setting of the office thermostat. She fights about employees being mistreated and overworked, and she constantly complains that her department is understaffed.

Victoria does not understand the need for, and effectiveness of, subtlety, diplomacy and patience in the workplace. She does not understand why political strategies at the workplace may be necessary in some instances. She does not understand that she actually might do better to selectively fight *certain* battles than to fight all of them.

She wants a promotion and does not understand why she does not get it. The job would require finesse and involves managing other people. It would require her to prioritize projects and issues. It would also require Victoria to understand how and when to pick her battles and to effectively manage other people's battles. Because of her history of picking *every* battle, management is simply not convinced that she could effectively handle those responsibilities.

*   *   *

Be aware that no one wants to be perceived as a constant complainer. No one wants to develop a reputation for being contrary or disagreeable; or as someone who is not a team player or who cannot get along with others. No one wants to be perceived as someone with a bad attitude. No one wants to be perceived as someone who is unreasonable or cannot distinguish between important issues which are worth fighting about and less significant ones which are not.

As the Victoria scenario illustrates, people who fight about every negative issue that arises at their workplace or who do not carefully and selectively pick their battles are likely to be perceived in these ways. Significantly, as is evidenced by Victoria's situation, those individuals are less likely to be effective in ultimately getting what they want, either for themselves or for others.

For these reasons, before taking on a particular battle at work, ask yourself what it is that you hope to gain by doing so. If picking the battle does not assist you in getting what you want, however that is defined, perhaps you should rethink whether that particular fight is worth fighting at all.

In addition, when you *do* selectively pick a battle, it should be for a good reason. Be prepared to articulate and defend that reason and to appeal to the sense of fairness in others through calm and intelligent discussion. If you *do* make conscious decisions about which battles to pick and which ones to avoid; *do* have good, well thought-out reasons for the ones you pick; and *are* well-prepared to defend those reasons, you are likely to appear to be reasonable and credible, which can only help you.

Having a reputation for being reasonable and credible at work will increase the likelihood that you will more respected by your supervisors and co-workers. It will also enhance your chances of winning the particular battle you are engaged in and ultimately of getting what you want out of the situation.

Finally, having a reputation for being reasonable and credible at work is an investment in your future at the organization. You will likely be perceived as a serious, even-handed, level-headed person who does not take a position unless there is substantial justification, which will increase the likelihood that you will be taken seriously in *future* battles that may need to be fought as well.

* * *

The bottom line is that the workplace, like life itself, is full of injustices. All of the wrongs that may exist in the workplace cannot necessarily be righted. People who try to right every wrong at the workplace can develop reputations as individuals who "cry wolf" too often, which may not ultimately serve their own best interests.

Remember, never lose sight of your goals and always try to engage in conduct which assists you in achieving them. Picking your battles carefully is just one more strategy designed to help you get what you ultimately want out of your workplace situation.

Avoid Being Inflammatory

Most of us have an instinct when we perceive ourselves as having been attacked at the workplace to "attack-back." How many of us, for example, have been chastised at work in front of others or have been on the receiving end of a stinging memo or note from a supervisor, customer or client? In those instances, how many of us have the instinct to respond in kind; to "vent" our negative energy or anger; or to insist upon sending up a stinging written reply?

Regardless of what our "instincts" might be in those situations, the fact is that responding in kind or responding in an inflammatory manner usually does not help to resolve most workplace conflicts. In fact, more often than not, it typically does nothing but add fuel to the fire; perpetuate the fight; and make matters worse.

The "Dueling E-Mail" Scenario

Consider the classic, modern example of the "dueling e-mails" or the "dueling memos." This scenario typically arises as follows. Nate receives a written memo, letter or e-mail message from Arnold that he perceives to be accusatory, untrue, misleading, or chastising. As is commonly the case in this type of situation, Nate feels compelled to respond in writing and while he is still angry from reading the message. His response is likely to be very pointed and is not likely to be productive in resolving the issue.

Once Nate responds, Arnold then feels compelled to respond to Nate's comments. Arnold's response is likely to be even more emotionally charged than his original memo or e-mail was. The e-mail/memo war is on and both parties will likely insist on getting in the last word.

* * *

The result of the dueling e-mail scenario is that both parties have now become highly inflamed. At this point, they are not only no closer to productively resolving their issue, but, in all likelihood, they have also angered and alienated each other to such a degree that they are actually *further away* from resolving the issue than they were before the memos were exchanged.

The "Honey/Vinegar" Approach

There is an old adage that people can catch more flies with honey than with vinegar. This certainly has relevant application to the emotionally charged workplace. A more inflammatory approach (the "vinegar") is more likely to make others defensive, angry and hostile. Once angered, few people think clearly, reasonably or objectively. In those situations, *no one* is likely to get what they want. By contrast, a reasonable, objective, calm approach (the "honey") to problem solving at the workplace not only tends to succeed more of the time in getting people what they ultimately want, but it also is more likely to make everyone's work experience more positive and productive.

Because you can catch more flies with honey than with vinegar, it is critically important *not* to give in to the "attack-back" instinct. Rather, it is particularly necessary in the face of supervisors, co-workers and others who appear to be on the attack that you *control* your anger and restrain yourself from fighting back in kind.

Remember, always be mindful of what you want, both in the short term and in the long term. In the case of the chastising supervisor or client, while you may feel better in the short run by venting your anger, telling your supervisor off, or responding aggressively, you might very well be shooting yourself in the foot in the long run.

No client or customer wants to be told that he is wrong or that you disagree with him, particularly when he is in the midst of venting anger himself. Doing so could increase the risk that he might take his business elsewhere. Similarly, most bosses do not want subordinates responding in kind. Doing so could increase the risk of losing one's job; losing a promotion or raise; or creating a lasting impression of being a complainer, a troublemaker and/or not a team player.

That is not to say that you should never make your opinion known. The suggestion here is merely that you (1) pick your spots for your battles selectively (in the manner and for all of the reasons discussed earlier in the Chapter); and (2) not respond to an already inflamed situation either by becoming inflamed yourself or by further inflaming others.

Other Strategies for Responding to Inflamed Persons at Work

What follows are several additional strategies designed (1) to assist you in getting what you want out of an already inflamed situation at work; and (2) to help you avoid increasing the level of emotional tension at work; making *yourself* more upset; making your supervisors or co-workers *more* upset; or making a workplace situation *more* inflamed.

Avoid Sending Written Responses Initially

Be aware, as a supervisor or employee yourself, that *sending* memos with highly charged language or speaking in too blunt or angry a tone is likely to offend people's sensibilities and make them much more defensive. Obviously, you are much less likely to get what you want from people if they feel offended or defensive.

You should also be aware that it is common for people to want to respond to a hostile communication immediately and in writing. They tend to feel a sense of unfairness and an overwhelming urge to respond in kind; to respond nastily; to go on "record"; and/or to "document their file," even though these types of strategies, particularly those involving an immediate, nasty, written response, are commonly not effective in getting people what they want.

Sometimes, a response in writing might be necessary or productive, but often it is not. Sometimes, all that a situation requires is that the issue be talked out between the sender of the message and the recipient. Sometimes, the best strategy to employ in these instances is to let the matter drop for the time being and pick up the discussion at a future point when the circumstances are calmer. In still other instances, it might be appropriate to let the issue die completely and not address it at all.

Perhaps the best strategy for responding to an employee whom you believe has "attacked" you is to retreat, regroup, and come up with a calmer, longer term strategy for addressing the issue in question. As was also noted earlier in the Chapter, there truly are very few things that *must* be addressed immediately.

When and How to Send Written Responses

It is virtually *never* advisable to send a *written* response to any disturbing or negative verbal or written communication that you receive at work if that response was written in the heat of the moment or while you were angry or upset. (It is also usually not advisable to respond, even verbally, to any angry message while you remain angry.) Written responses are particularly dangerous because those documents could become part of your permanent employment record and it is very likely that, after you calm down and rethink your response, you may regret having sent it.

If you need to vent your frustrations or release some hostile, pent-up emotion, it might be productive for you to jot down some private notes which express how you feel. In extreme circumstances, you may even want to *prepare* a *draft* of a written response. (Writing down a response or summary of your feelings about workplace situations can calm you down and may even make you feel better.)

However, do not make the mistake of *sending* a writing of this sort to anyone at work simply because it may make you feel better in the short run. If it is actually sent, it is likely to inflame others further and not help you get what you want or make your workplace situation more positive in the long run. Under those circumstances, it is strongly recommended that you show no one at work your notes and do not *send* any written response of this nature until, at a minimum, you have a substantial opportunity to calm down and reflect upon the advisability of doing so.

After you have jotted down your thoughts, reconsider whether a written response to the situation, or any response at all, is even warranted. (Be aware that this period of "reflection" might be hours, days or even weeks, depending on the circumstances, the severity of the situation and/or the need to act relatively promptly.)

If you still believe that a *written* response in *some* form *is* warranted and necessary, it is very likely that you will want to (or should) tone down the original draft substantially before sending it. Try to rewrite it in a tone which is more positive, resolution-oriented and productive, and perhaps less aggressive and offensive. (Responding in a less angry, more professional tone will also be less likely to upset the other party.)

Further, make sure that your written or other response is sent or communicated in a moment of calm deliberation, not a moment of lingering anger. Remember, once your response is out there in the workplace in whatever form it takes, you cannot take it back. To some degree, you also lose control at that point over who in the organization might see or hear about it.

Finally, with respect to who else might see a document that you generate, note also that it is not uncommon for people to have an instinct to provide copies to a wide variety of people at their organization. Be advised that being over-inclusive about who receives a communication of this type can have the effect of upsetting others who are not presently involved in the situation, which is the last thing you need in your efforts to try to resolve the problem.

To the extent that you can control who receives copies of these types of communications, you should make every effort to do so. Think about who, if anyone, should get copies *before* you send them. Think about who really has a "need to know" about the issue and/or about your response. Try to limit the distribution list to only those people.

* * *

In short, if you are looking to make your work experience more positive, try not to inflame an already incendiary situation by adding fuel to the proverbial fire. You are far more likely to get what you want by remaining cool, calm and patient; by not reacting to any workplace situation when you are upset or angry; and by not causing others to be upset or angry either.

Seek Positive Reinforcement

It is extremely important for everyone in every workplace to seek and get positive reinforcement for the work that they perform. Positive reinforcement keeps people motivated and increases the likelihood of making their work experiences more positive and pleasant.

Why Supervisors Don't Always Provide Proper Reinforcement

Unfortunately, supervisors and managers often fail to inform their employees that they are doing a good job. Many supervisors can be quick to criticize, but slow to praise.

Some supervisors can be very demanding, for example. It is their *expectation* that their employees will satisfy those demands and succeed in their jobs. In those instances, where employees *do* satisfy those demands, the supervisors tend to believe that positive reinforcement is not necessary because the employees are only doing what they are *supposed* to do. On the other hand, when those employees fail to meet those demands, those same supervisors will not hesitate to criticize.

Other supervisors may simply lose sight of how important positive reinforcement is. They make the mistake of assuming that their employees believe that "no news is good news." They assume that their employees understand that, if they have not heard anything negative about a particular job or project, or about their performance generally, the employees will somehow "know" that they are in fact doing a good job.

Still other supervisors may not know what their employees are working on or what those employees may have accomplished recently. These supervisors can be busy people with many responsibilities. Sometimes they supervise many individuals. They can get distracted and lose track of what their people are working on.

Look for Ways to Reinforce Yourself

If your supervisors do not provide you with appropriate or sufficient positive reinforcement at work for whatever reason, or even if they do, it would serve you well to find ways to positively reinforce yourself. Doing so will assist you in your continuing effort to feel positive about yourself; the work that you do; and the contribution that you make at your job.

There are a number of ways to seek and find positive reinforcement for yourself at work. What follows are some suggested strategies for doing so.

Take Pride in Your Accomplishments

One way to positively reinforce yourself is to take pride in your accomplishments. Compliment yourself on your successes. Praise yourself for your strengths. If you achieved a good result or reached a particular goal, whether or not anyone else at your workplace acknowledges it or even knows about it, periodically remind yourself that you achieved the result or reached the goal.

Try not to wait for someone else to recognize or acknowledge the accomplishment. For any number of reasons, that may not happen and you may find yourself being very disappointed and even disillusioned at times. What will help to keep you positive and confident in your abilities and your accomplishments is to make a point of acknowledging your strengths and achievements for yourself.

(Be careful in this regard, however. It is equally important for you to be honest with yourself about, and provide yourself with a fair assessment of, your weak areas at work as well. Many employees have a false sense of their strengths; think that they are strong performers in all areas; and are shocked when they are criticized for any reason. In order to truly be positively reinforced and develop confidence in your true strengths, you need to be realistic in your self-evaluations.)

Acknowledge Reinforcing Remarks from Non-Supervisors

Another way to seek positive reinforcement at work is to pay attention to the positive feedback that you receive during the course of a week, month or year from colleagues, clients, co-workers, and/or customers. These comments may be isolated and may not seem that important when made or in the context in which they are made, but they are nevertheless an important form of positive reinforcement.

Try not to dismiss these positive comments out of hand simply because they did not come directly from your supervisor or manager. These types of comments can help you feel more positive about yourself and the work that you do.

Consider the following example. Barbara works very hard and achieves excellent results on a consistent basis for her employer. She never complains and does whatever she is told. She does not make herself very visible at work. She can always be counted on in a pinch and frequently sacrifices personal commitments in her continued efforts to show loyalty and commitment to her employer. Many of her co-workers respect her; believe that she is always well-prepared; and believe that she consistently does a good job.

Barbara's supervisors, however, take her for granted; take advantage of her loyalty and her good nature; are quick to criticize her when she makes a mistake; and rarely compliment her on her dedication or work performance.

When a co-worker who is in an objective position to observe her performance tells her that, despite what people may or may not say to her about her work performance, she is in fact an "extremely valuable asset" to the organization, Barbara should take those comments seriously. In her efforts to make her work situation more positive and make herself feel more confident about her work, it might be productive and positively reinforcing for her to periodically remind herself of this comment (or others like it that she may receive from time to time).

*   *   *

Consider the additional example of Peter. He is very competent and talented in his own right, but works for a boss who is quite arrogant and who commonly condescends to employees and customers alike. One day, one of the organization's customers whom Peter deals with on a regular basis tells him that she would rather speak to him than his boss because she "just did not feel like being patronized today."

Peter should take great comfort in that remark. The message that this customer communicated to Peter is that she likes him, respects him, and prefers to deal with him directly rather than have to contend with the arrogance and condescension of his boss.

Self-Promotion

Still another method for seeking positive reinforcement at work is "self-promotion." As noted above, your supervisors may not be aware of what you are working on or may not know about some of your recent successes or accomplishments. Do not assume that supervisors and managers *are* aware either of what you are working on or of your accomplishments, and have simply chosen not to acknowledge them. It is very likely in some instances that they simply do *not* know.

It is up to you to make sure that your supervisors and managers, and/or other persons whom you perceive to be your supporters in your organization, *do* know what you are working on and what a good job you are doing. It is your responsibility to "promote" yourself in your organization to the fullest extent necessary to make individuals who need to know fully aware of what it is that you have done.

Try not to be shy about pointing out your positive attributes to those who might not be aware of them. Although self-promotion may not come naturally to some people, it is important and sometimes necessary to make sure that the individuals who need to know *are* aware of what you are doing and what you have accomplished. Perhaps the only reason that you are *not* getting any positive reinforcement from your supervisor is that he or she simply is unaware of all of the things that you have done.

In addition, try to make sure that you take credit and get credit for your accomplishments. If you do not, perhaps you will not be credited for the work or, worse yet, someone else will attempt to take the credit for himself or herself.

Finally, pick well chosen spots to "toot your own horn" if necessary. It is not uncommon at the workplace, for example, for particularly assertive individuals to boastfully tell anyone who will listen about how "great," "skilled," or "accomplished" they are. We all know of individuals in our various workplaces who do this. What can be somewhat surprising and even remarkable about these individuals is how often their audience, including supervisors and managers, might actually believe the "buzz" that they create about themselves.

Everyone is capable of creating some level of positive "buzz" about themselves at work. Be aware, however, that it is not necessary to be *boastful* in order to make your supervisors aware of your accomplishments and talents. Many individuals have been equally successful in talking up their strengths in a way which is positive and subtle and neither obnoxious nor overbearing. As a general rule, most people will be most successful in "tooting their horns" when they do so at times, in a manner, in a context, and in a style which is most natural to them and with which they feel most comfortable.

Don't Forget to Laugh

Sometimes people take themselves and their jobs too seriously. Despite the demands and pressures of your job, make sure that you take some time to laugh at work every now and then.

That is not to say, of course, that work is not serious. Work *is* serious and, for the most part, should be taken seriously.

However, just because work is usually serious does not mean that you cannot have some fun and enjoy the environment in which you work and/or the people with whom you work. Surely, during the course of a typical workday or workweek, *something* will happen which is light and out of the ordinary.

Consider the following example. George has worked as an art director for two advertising agencies. Both agencies have the same types of demanding clients. Both work on the same types of big campaigns, where large amounts of money are at stake. Both are faced with the same deadline pressures. The people in both agencies are hard working and put in extremely late hours at times. The pressure of constantly coming up with creative ideas exists at both places.

Why is it then that George greatly enjoyed his work experience at the second agency, but did not enjoy his experience at the first agency at all? George would say that the environment at the second agency was much more positive, pleasant, and enjoyable than at the first. The work environment at the second agency was much looser and George simply enjoyed the company of the people at the second agency better.

At the second agency, George could be playful from time to time. In fact, he and others, including owners and managers of the agency, commonly *were* playful, particularly when working late at night.

At the second agency, a number of people kept small toys at their desks and others had standing invitations to play with them when they were so moved. In addition, the agency routinely bought dinner for those working late. Employees and managers alike would often eat together as a group, sharing personal jokes and stories. The agency also purchased a small, free-standing basketball hoop, which was set up in a common area. It was not uncommon, particularly during late-night work sessions or during exceptionally stressful workdays, for employees and managers alike to take a few minutes to shoot baskets to relieve the stress of a given moment as well.

The management philosophy of the second agency was to *encourage* employees to be playful, obviously within reason, within legal parameters and in manners which were unlikely to offend anyone's sensibilities. It was the belief of management at the second agency that, if employees could be kept fresh, interested, and enthused about the work, they were more likely to remain motivated and, ultimately, to be more productive.

*   *   *

As the George example makes clear, sometimes you need to just take a step back and, rather than fight or inflame a supervisor or customer, take a moment to laugh at the silliness of a given situation. As long as you are not exploiting someone's weaknesses; laughing at someone else's expense; acting in a mean-spirited way or in a manner which others find distasteful or offensive; or undermining the confidence of those who have entrusted you to perform a service for them, there is no reason why you cannot allow yourself to laugh at appropriate moments while at work.

Of course, it is important to understand that not all situations at work are laughable. Depending upon the type of job you have or work environment you are in, some work situations, like, for example, those arising in the health care field, are obviously particularly serious and need to be treated with the appropriate degree of respect.

However, as a general principle, the concepts of hard work, being productive, satisfying clients, and meeting sales goals, for example, are not necessarily mutually exclusive with the idea of laughing and loosening up at work. The basic truth is that laughing is fun and can relieve stress. Laughing might even relax you. If you and your co-workers or supervisors can bond by sharing a light moment together, you might find that everyone involved is motivated to work harder and be more productive.

*   *   *

In short, try to lighten up every once in awhile. You just might find that laughing and loosening up, or being encouraged to do so by your supervisors or upper management at your organization, could help make your work environment a bit more positive and pleasant; motivate you to work even harder; or be a refreshing diversion which makes you even more productive. You might just find that laughing is a ticket toward making your work situation a win-win situation for everyone.

CHAPTER 6

Image Is Everything (Almost)

"Image is everything" is a phrase that we have all heard in many different contexts in our lives. Organizations, famous athletes, movie personalities, and other celebrities hire publicists to create an "image" about themselves in the minds of the public. Sometimes organizations hire particular celebrities to endorse their products and to assist them in creating a particular kind of "image." We are all familiar, for example, with the "image" that certain soft drink companies or athletic apparel companies try to project.

In the everyday work world, image is equally important, albeit on a much smaller scale. Although it might be somewhat of an overstatement to conclude that "image is *everything*" at the workplace, it certainly would be a mistake to conclude that "image" is *not* an important factor in workplace politics. The truth is that you are more likely to get what you want and have a positive work experience if, among other things, you can create a positive "image" of yourself.

Consider the following example. Irene and Ellen both work for the same organization in comparable positions. Ellen has been with the organization longer. She is highly competent and has even been described by some as "brilliant" at her job. She does not believe in workplace politics. She believes that she should be judged on her accomplishments alone, which are substantial. She is shy, a bit awkward socially, and tends to keep to herself at work.

Irene is highly competent as well and has many accomplishments in her own right. She, however, is not at all shy about telling co-workers, supervisors, support staff and customers about her accomplishments every chance she gets. She spends a good deal of time convincing people that she truly is a star.

*   *   *

When the time comes for one of these individuals to be promoted, guess who gets the promotion? It is Irene, of course. This is a perfect example of how image building can work effectively for you and how the failure to pay attention to image building sometimes can be quite costly.

What Does "Image" Mean in the Workplace Context?

What is "image," as it relates to your job? In short, it is how others *perceive* you.

Consider the following questions, in an effort to understand what your present "image" in your workplace might be. Are you well-liked in your workplace, particularly by persons who are in positions to make decisions that could affect your job and career? Do your co-workers trust and respect you? Are you considered to be a "brown-noser" or a "snitch"? Are you perceived as a winner? Are you perceived as someone who has a positive attitude toward your job? Are you perceived as lazy? Are you perceived as someone who makes many mistakes? Are you perceived as someone who complains too much; someone who looks for excuses for not getting work done; or someone who is not likely to take the blame for something that you did wrong?

*   *   *

Whether or not you believe that the workplace perceptions about you are accurate, truthful or fair, and whether you like it or not, the basic truths are that (1) people *do* develop perceptions about you; and (2) image *is* a critically important factor at any workplace in helping you to get what you want. Most of us can maximize the likelihood of making our work experiences more positive, productive and pleasant by creating a positive image for ourselves in our workplaces.

What Image Do You Want to Project about Yourself?

It is important to remember that, at least to some degree, you *can* control and create your own image at your workplace. You need to decide, however, exactly what image it is that you want to project.

Consider the following additional questions in your effort to determine what you would *like* your workplace image to be and why. Do you want to be everyone's friend? Do you want to be perceived as the compassionate manager? Do you want to be perceived as someone who works hard and tries to stay out of the fray? Do you want to be perceived as someone who is tough, but fair?

These questions cannot be effectively answered in the abstract, and the image you desire to create for yourself can vary from job to job and organization to organization. In determining what image you want to project for yourself, therefore, you may also need to consider the type of job you have; the personalities of the people who supervise you and who run your organization; and the type of organization that you work for.

Consider the example of lawyers who perform different types of legal functions for their clients. Sydney is a trial lawyer. In litigation, clients expect their attorneys to be very aggressive on their behalf. For that reason, it would be useful for Sydney to create an image for herself with her clients, co-workers, employers, and opposing lawyers as someone who passionately believes in her causes and who will fight for her clients at all costs.

By contrast, Paul is an advice lawyer. He rarely appears in court and makes his living by trying to find creative solutions for keeping his clients out of trouble. The image that Paul may want to project to his clients and colleagues is that he is smart, level-headed, sensible, objective, and creative, particularly when faced with the pressure of potentially adverse circumstances for his clients.

How to Create a Positive Image at Work

There are a number of strategies that you can employ to help create a positive image for yourself at work. Several of those have already been explored elsewhere in this book. In Chapter 4, for example, creating a perception that you work hard, get good results and are a team player was addressed. Similarly, in Chapter 5, creating perceptions based upon your ability to make sure that everyone at work knows what you are working on and about your accomplishments was discussed. What follows are some additional suggested strategies for creating a positive image for yourself at work.

Creating Positive First and Ongoing Impressions

When you start a new job with a new organization, or when you are moved into a different position or department in your existing organization, it is vital to make a good first impression. If you create an initial impression, for example, that you are not hard working, it may be difficult later on to reverse that perception, no matter how hard you try. To some extent, first impressions created at the workplace can be lasting.

In addition, *maintaining* a positive image over some length of time at work can be equally important. We have all heard the expression, "What have you done for me lately?" To that extent, image building is, and should be, an ongoing process.

Those who are most successful in creating and maintaining positive images for themselves are constantly working on their workplace images. The goal in doing so is that when a mistake occurs or a downturn hits their organization, these individuals have done as much as they possibly can to insulate themselves from being fired, demoted, or criticized. Those people who do not continue to work on their image over time at work run the risk of having their images shattered.

Consider the following example. Marcia has been working for the same organization for years. She has developed an excellent reputation for doing high-quality work. She has created a positive image of working hard and of being a team player over a prolonged period of time with a variety of supervisors and co-workers.

She is then transferred to work directly with Thomas, a supervisor for whom she has not worked previously and who, unbeknownst to her at the time, appears to have the ear of some very influential managers in the organization. Marcia is confident that other supervisors with whom she has previously worked will inform Thomas of her prior accomplishments and that her positive image in the organization will remain intact.

Thomas, however, turns out to be unreasonably demanding and to have a reputation among those who work with him as being quite difficult. He pushes Marcia and others who work for him well beyond any reasonable working hours. It quickly becomes evident to Marcia that no amount or quality of work will satisfy Thomas. Unfortunately, she is assigned to him for a six-month project and cannot be reassigned until the project is completed.

Marcia then proceeds to work an average of 13 to 15 hours per day, as well as nearly every weekend day, during the six-month period, in an effort to get all of the work that Thomas has assigned to her done. Given that schedule, she is unable to network with or do any work for any other managers in the organization during that time period.

She is also unable to communicate to anyone other than Thomas about how hard she is working and has no time to even complain about how demanding Thomas is as a supervisor. After a few months of working with Thomas, he becomes the only supervisor in the entire organization who has any meaningful impression of Marcia based upon her *current* work.

Despite all of Marcia's efforts, Thomas still develops the impression that she is not willing to work hard enough, because she took a few days off during the six-month project. To make matters worse, Thomas spreads the word among a number of managers in the organization that Marcia is not a team player and is not willing to do whatever is necessary to get a project done, neglecting to mention how hard she has been working.

* * *

Because Marcia had fallen "out of the loop" with other managers in the organization and had failed to maintain her positive image in the organization during the time that she worked for Thomas, Thomas was able to successfully tarnish Marcia's image despite her prior successes and her prior reputation. This example illustrates that, no matter how hard you may work to create a positive image at the workplace, doing so needs to be an ongoing process.

Perceptions about Work Habits During the Ordinary Workday

During the workday, your supervisors need to *see* you and need to develop a perception that you *are* in fact working. Be careful to avoid certain behaviors which can create a negative impression that you are not.

Consider the following questions, in an effort to determine whether you have a negative image or have created a negative impression on others at your workplace. Do you take exceedingly long lunches? Do you have a habit of coming in late to work? Do you commonly leave work early? Is your supervisor aware of the amount of time you spend away from your job during your typical workday? Are you often on the phone, even though your job does not require you to be on the phone? Is there a perception that you spend your time and the organization's money making personal phone calls while at work? Are you often on the Internet for non-work reasons during the course of an average workday? Is there a perception that people gravitate to your office or work station and that there is too much socializing, rather than working, going on during those times?

If you answered "yes" to any of these questions, you may inadvertently and unnecessarily be creating a negative image for yourself at work. Be aware that these types of activities can leave negative impressions and try to minimize the amount of time you spend at work engaging in them.

"Face Time" During Off Hours

Many people assume that their employers are most concerned about their employees getting the work done; getting it done on time; and getting it done right. If asked, those individuals might say that their employers do not care *how* or *when* they get the work done, as long as they get it done. Those same individuals may end up working at home or working late nights, early mornings, or weekends, without their supervisors knowing *when* they are working and/or without getting "credit" for working those hours.

While getting the work done timely and properly is obviously very important, making sure that people *see* you *at* work, particularly if you are working off hours, can be equally important. It confirms the perception that you *are* in fact working hard and aids in developing your overall positive image.

Consider the following example. It is common practice at Yvonne's organization for most of the supervisors and managers to work a half-day or more on Saturdays. It is part of the work culture. Even those who get most of their work done during the week commonly show up at work on Saturdays because there is a *perception* in this organization that, if managers are not working on Saturdays, they are not working very hard. For this reason, Yvonne makes a point of coming in to work on most Saturdays.

* * *

This example illustrates the importance of developing positive perceptions about yourself at work. If you are working hard, the last thing that you want is for the power players at work to have somehow developed the impression that you are not.

One strategy to ensure that your supervisors and other decision makers in your organization *are* aware of the hours you work is to leave your work station every once in awhile in the early mornings, late into the evenings or on weekends while you are there and walk through the office or workplace so that people *know* that you *are* there during those times. Doing so may increase the likelihood that you will get "credit" for doing the work, as well as make it more likely that you will be *perceived* as working hard and as a team player who is willing to sacrifice some of your personal life for the good of the organization.

Note that not every organization requires any of its employees to work overtime, early mornings, late evenings, or weekends. In addition, not every organization has enough work to justify people working during those hours. For those organizations that do, however, putting in "face time" can help your overall image.

(A word of caution is appropriate here, however. Make sure that putting in "face time" during off hours is not *only* about the "face time." The purpose of "face time" is to show people that you *are* in fact *working* during those off hours. If you spend an entire Saturday at work socializing with people just to put in "face time," for example, a perception might develop that you are *not* working hard. For that reason, as long as you are *at* work during those off hours, try to make sure that you actually *do* some work during those times and that others actually *see* you working.)

* * *

Remember, a critical aspect of image development is to create an impression in others that you are working; that you work hard; that you get positive results; that you are a team player; and that you will do whatever is necessary to get the job done.

PART THREE

Working and Playing
Well with Others

CHAPTER 7

A Message for Supervisors and Managers: Suggestions for Keeping Your Employees Motivated

This Chapter is directed specifically at supervisors and managers and is based upon the premise that they want to motivate their employees. Presumably, supervisors and managers understand that, if employees can be kept happy, relaxed, positive, and confident, they will be more motivated to work hard, which in turn will make them more productive, which in turn will make the supervisors and managers look good; bring more money into their organizations; and/or bring more visibility to those organizations.

The purpose of this Chapter is to provide some basic insights about non-managerial employees in an effort to assist those supervisors and managers in making their employees more productive. What follows are common pitfalls that supervisors and managers often fall into when attempting to manage and motivate their employees and some suggested strategies for best resolving those issues so that employees, supervisors and organizations all can benefit.

Develop a Better Understanding of What Motivates Employees

In order to keep employees motivated, managers need to develop a better understanding of their employees and the effects that their actions can and often do have on their employees. Toward that end, they may need to be educated about *how* and *what* employees think and what they are likely *to be* thinking (and/or how they are likely to act or react) in response to supervisors' and managers' words, actions, directions, omissions, tones and body language.

Unfortunately, it is common at the workplace for supervisors and managers not to be sufficiently tuned in to these issues. Sometimes, they get too busy and become distracted by their own immediate pressures. Sometimes, supervisors lose sight of their ongoing need to understand exactly what their employees are likely experiencing at work themselves.

Supervisors' failures in these areas can of course have negative effects on their employees. For example, supervisors and managers constantly need to be aware that they should choose their words and courses of action carefully, to avoid inadvertently hurting employees' feelings and/or pushing their negative buttons. When this happens, employees can and commonly *do* become less confident, less relaxed, more intimidated, more angry, and/or more resentful. The less positive overall that employees feel either about themselves, their managers, or their workplace situation, the less job satisfaction and motivation they are likely to have.

It must be emphasized that it does not matter whether supervisors or managers *know* that they are causing or *intend* to cause employees to be demoralized or humiliated. Commonly, supervisors and managers are *not* aware that their words, actions, or management styles have the effect of making their employees feel unappreciated. However, the effect on the employee is the same whether supervisors and managers are aware of the consequences of their actions or not.

The bottom line is that supervisors and managers need to be mindful of these issues in order to effectively get what they ultimately want: employees who feel satisfied with their jobs and themselves so that they will be motivated to work at peak efficiency and productivity.

Avoid Falling Victim to the "Eye-of-the-Beholder Syndrome"

A common trap that supervisors and managers (and people in the world generally) sometimes fall into is the "Eye-of-the-Beholder Syndrome." The "Eye-of-the-Beholder Syndrome" involves a basic assumption that most people go through life looking at the world through their own unique "filter." What this means is that, if left to their own devices, most people, including most supervisors and managers, will view events and judge people based upon their own life and workplace experiences, a perspective that they can easily understand and accept. In short, people tend to ascribe characteristics to others, and view others' goals and agendas, as being similar to their own.

How many people do you know, for example, who think that their friends and colleagues are all exactly like they are? How many people do you know who seek solace from, and tend to gravitate to, other individuals who think the way they think; act the way they act; and are motivated by the same things that they are motivated by?

In the workplace, those supervisors and managers who fall victim to the "Eye-of-the-Beholder Syndrome" tend to believe that their employees have the same goals and agendas either as each other or as the managers themselves. For example, the person who plays "fast and loose" with information assumes that everyone does. Similarly, the workplace manipulator typically assumes that everyone, like him, has an agenda.

Unfortunately, that is commonly not the case. Supervisors and managers need to develop an understanding that people are different and that different people can be, and frequently are, motivated by different things and in different ways. One way to avoid the "Eye-of-the-Beholder" trap is for supervisors and managers to (1) "get inside their employees' heads"; (2) try to understand how each individual employee separately thinks; and (3) *never* assume that everyone who works for them *is* alike, is like them, or *is* motivated by the same things, no matter how much their instincts might tell them that they are.

Consider the following example. Caroline and Ellen are business partners. Their single bond is their common desire to make a lot of money.

They have 100 employees working for them. They have not taken the time to get to know most of their employees as individuals. They do not have a sense of what motivates most of their employees.

Caroline and Ellen have one strategy and one strategy only for motivating their employees: pay them greater than market salaries for their jobs. Their view of the world (their "Eye-of-the-Beholder") is that "money is what motivates us, so money is what must motivate everyone."

Unfortunately, much to their surprise and chagrin, many of their employees are *not* motivated by money to the same degree that they are. For that reason, if they are not careful and do not take the time to figure out what *does* motivate their employees individually, Caroline and Ellen are likely to find themselves in the midst of a morale crisis, with many unmotivated and unsatisfied employees.

* * *

What Caroline and Ellen need to understand and recognize in the above example is that not everyone is equally motivated by money. Some people are motivated by power. Some people are motivated by increased responsibilities. Some people are motivated by positive reinforcement or feedback. Some people are motivated by a desire to help others. As a result, one motivation strategy is not likely be successful for *any* entire group or organization of employees.

*   *   *

For these reasons, supervisors and managers need to learn what *each and every* employee individually wants from his or her job and what motivates each person individually. This is obviously a difficult, tedious, and time-consuming task, but one well worth taking on. Remember, everyone has different goals and agendas. The best way to motivate each individual is to understand what motivates each individual.

Your Employees Are More Perceptive than You Might Think

Another common pitfall that supervisors and managers tend to fall victim to is that they tend to underestimate their employees. Many managers think, for example, that, because in some cases they (1) supervise; (2) have power over; (3) make decisions affecting; (4) make more money than; (5) are older than; or (6) have more formal education than their employees, they are somehow "smarter" than or "superior" to those employees.

These are common and potentially dangerous misconceptions for supervisors and managers to have. All people at the workplace are capable of sensing and observing to varying degrees. Everyone picks up on stray remarks and body language from others. Everyone perceives and makes judgments based on those perceptions on a daily basis. It would behoove most supervisors and managers to understand that education levels, intelligence levels and perceptiveness levels come in all shapes and sizes.

As is true in life generally, everyone has their strengths and weaknesses. Just because a supervisor or manager may have more relevant education and experience than his or her employees in some areas does not mean that he or she is more intelligent or intuitive than those employees in other areas.

Most employees are more perceptive and intelligent than their supervisors give them credit for. One of the biggest mistakes that supervisors and managers can make is to fail to give sufficient credit to their employees' abilities to observe events around them and make intelligent judgments based on those perceptions.

Take the "fast and loose" supervisor at work, for example. He likes to pull the wool over people's eyes and believes that he is always successful at it. He *is* skilled at it and *has been* successful in many instances at doing it. He convinces himself, however, that he is infallible in this regard and that no one can see through his deceptions. He is confident that his employees could not possibly figure out that his decisions, words or actions are motivated by ego or self-interest; that he has an agenda; what his agenda might be; or that he is not being truthful about the reasons he offers for his actions or directions.

In many instances, "Mr. Fast and Loose" could not be more mistaken and misguided. Just because employees do not always choose to call him on his motivations does not mean that they are unaware of them. Sometimes, they might be afraid of losing their jobs. Sometimes, they might be stroking his ego. Sometimes, they may be carefully picking their own battles. Sometimes, they may just want to be left alone to do their jobs and not get involved in the boss' politics or manipulations. Sometimes, they may be manipulating him, although he may be too blind and lacking in perception himself to realize that his employees could possibly be as smart as he is in some areas.

What "Mr. Fast and Loose" (and other managers like him) *does* typically do when he underestimates the intelligence or perceptiveness levels of his employees is to alienate those employees. Most people *do* see through these things, if not immediately, certainly over the long run.

Once employees perceive that they or their intelligence level is being underestimated, they are likely to feel insulted and humiliated; become angry and resentful; feel used and patronized; and/or perhaps even *believe* that they *are* in fact stupid or inferior to their bosses. How motivated are employees likely to be under those circumstances?

* * *

The bottom line here is to have faith in the intelligence and competence of the employees whom supervisors and managers have chosen to do their jobs and try not to underestimate them. Employees sense that more often than most supervisors and managers realize, which is likely to have a debilitating effect on their morale.

Be Mindful of the Power/Influence that You Wield

Supervisors and managers sometimes do not realize how much power they wield; how impressionable their employees might be; and the dramatic effects that even their simplest and perhaps most innocent comments, actions, or inactions, can have on their employees. Obviously, managers need to be sensitive to these issues to avoid mistakenly engaging in conduct which could hurt their employees' feelings or cause them to be unmotivated to do their work.

Consider the following example. Melanie is a supervisor for a large company, which occupies twenty-five floors of a high-rise office building. She works on the forty-second floor of the building, as does Rhonda, one of the employees in Melanie's charge.

One morning, Melanie and Rhonda get on an elevator at the same time on the ground floor of their office building. They are the only two people in the elevator. Rhonda greets Melanie with a warm "Good Morning." Melanie not only does not respond to Rhonda in kind, but also does not look at or even acknowledge

Rhonda at all. The two of them ride up in the elevator alone in silence for twenty floors.

On the twenty-first floor, Ted, another supervisor for the company and a colleague of Melanie's, gets on the elevator. Although he does not directly supervise Rhonda, he knows her and greets both Melanie and Rhonda by saying "Good Morning." Both Rhonda and Melanie respond to him in kind. Melanie and Ted then commence a discussion about some business-related issues. Ted smiles at Rhonda during this brief exchange, but Melanie continues to ignore Rhonda. The three of them ride up to the forty-second floor of the building, continuing with this dynamic in place.

* * *

Ask yourself the following questions. Who would Rhonda be more motivated to work for, Melanie or Ted? In addition, what would Rhonda likely be feeling in response to Melanie's complete brush-off?

First, it seems obvious that Rhonda would be more inclined if she had the choice to work with Ted. He was gracious in his demeanor toward Rhonda, as opposed to Melanie, who refused to even acknowledge her existence.

Second, in response to Melanie's behavior, Rhonda is likely to wonder whether Melanie even knows who she is, even though Rhonda works in Melanie's department. She is likely to have hurt feelings. She is likely to think that Melanie is a snob. She might feel angry. She certainly is likely to interpret Melanie's actions as showing a lack of respect for Rhonda as an employee and/or as a person, which in turn might make her feel less confident in her abilities or less worthy as a human being. In any event, she is certainly likely to be less motivated to work or perform her work functions well for Melanie in the future.

* * *

The point of the Melanie/Rhonda/Ted scenario is to serve as a reminder to supervisors and managers that they are bosses and that they tend to wield more power and influence than they may realize. In order to maximize the effectiveness and motivation levels of their employees, supervisors and managers need to be aware (and constantly remind themselves) of the effects that their actions and comments *could have* on others. Their opinions and actions could shape how their employees perceive themselves, both at work and in life generally. Supervisors and managers are urged to take this responsibility seriously in their efforts not only to avoid hurting people's feelings unnecessarily, but also to ensure that their employees remain motivated to assist them.

The Carrot and the Stick

Consider the proverbial sports coach who yells and tries to intimidate her players. That coach believes that her players are motivated to perform at their peak levels by the fear of negative consequences that she instills in them.

Similarly, in the workplace, some supervisors believe that they get more productivity out of employees whom they hit with the proverbial "stick" than those whom they dangle a "carrot" in front of. However, while the "stick" approach may work in some instances in the short run, most employees are much more motivated, more positive, and more productive over the long haul when supervisors offer rewards (the "carrots") for stellar performance rather than criticisms or negative incentives (the "sticks"), particularly when excessive, for poor performance.

Supervisors need to understand that, for most employees, yelling and nastiness make them feel humiliated, angry and unmotivated. For these reasons, supervisors should try to avoid being snide, sarcastic, vicious, mean or personal in their management styles; and should try to avoid making any comments or criticisms which really have more to do with supervisor egos than with an employee's work performance.

Consider the following remarks made by supervisors toward their employees: (1) "I don't know where you got your training, but I am unsatisfied with your performance"; (2) "Your performance 'sucks'"; and (3) "This strategy is 'dopey.'" How motivated are the employees who were on the receiving end of those remarks likely to be?

In addition, how motivated is an employee likely to be in response to a supervisor who throws a phone across a room in anger over a mistake that the employee made? Further, how motivated is an employee likely to be after her supervisor loudly criticizes her in a corridor for all co-workers to hear and see?

The truth is that employees faced with these kinds of "stick-like" comments and actions are *not* likely to want to work hard for these supervisors. In fact, these types of comments and actions typically have exactly the opposite effect. Employees who receive these comments and/or are subjected to these types of actions are likely to remain unmotivated to work and can remain completely demoralized for days, weeks and sometimes even months afterward. Clearly, if supervisors were *aware* that their actions would have such unmotivating effects, one would hope that they would avoid such behaviors.

*　*　*

Remember, the goal is to provide incentives for individuals to work hard and perform well for their supervisors, managers and organizations. These negative strategies usually are not productive; are not positively reinforcing; and are not particularly motivating.

Communicate with Your Employees

Sometimes, in order to motivate employees, supervisors and managers need to communicate effectively with them. The failure to communicate clearly, directly, and positively with employees can cause negative responses from them as well, which in some instances can irreparably damage their working relationships with their supervisors.

Consider the following example. Teresa formerly worked as a manager for a large company. She reported directly to Sylvia, a Vice President for the company. During the time that she worked for the company, Teresa was under the impression that she had a close working relationship with Sylvia.

The company decided to eliminate the division for which Teresa worked. This meant that, unless she could be placed elsewhere in the overall organization, Teresa would be laid off along with dozens of others in her division. Although Sylvia was able to keep her job, she was unable to find jobs within the organization for Teresa and others like her after the layoff, despite her best efforts.

Unfortunately, Sylvia never communicated with Teresa that she tried to set her up elsewhere in the organization. In fact, once the layoff list was announced, Sylvia never communicated with Teresa at all. She was embarrassed that she did not have enough clout to save Teresa's job or to get her placed elsewhere in the organization. Despite their close relationship before the layoffs were announced, Sylvia went out of her way between the time of the announcement and the effective date of the layoffs to *avoid* interacting with Teresa at all.

This action was misinterpreted by Teresa. Because Sylvia never communicated to Teresa either that she tried to place Teresa or that she was embarrassed that she failed in doing so, Teresa did not understand Sylvia's change in behavior toward her. She misinterpreted Sylvia's actions as being a lack of support and her feelings were badly hurt.

In fact, Teresa was so personally angered by Sylvia's response to her after the layoff announcements that she ultimately brought a lawsuit against the company after her layoff. She claimed in the lawsuit that the company owed her additional compensation which Sylvia herself, on behalf of the company, had promised. The company ultimately expended large sums of money defending against Teresa's allegations.

* * *

Consider the additional example of Zoe, a mid-level manager who was passed over for promotion. She was under the impression that she was not only being considered, but that she was the likely candidate to receive the promotion. In fact, she turned down several job offers, expecting to get the promotion. At no time did her supervisor sit her down and have a candid and constructive discussion with her about her future limits with the organization or about her own limitations.

She did not get the promotion. She was never informed, either before the promotion decision was announced or after the decision was made known, as to why she did not get it. Nor were there ever any discussions with her regarding why the person who received the promotion was a better candidate than she was.

This complete lack of communication was humiliating for Zoe. She was hurt and embarrassed. She felt betrayed and used. She felt as if she were not part of the team and that she was not considered to be a valuable or meaningful contributor to the organization. She felt very unappreciated and not respected professionally or personally, and she did not feel very positive about herself personally after the announcement was made. Her motivation and productivity levels from that point forward decreased dramatically.

* * *

A lesson can be learned about supervisor communication from the cases of both Teresa and Zoe. In both cases, communication clearly could have and would have made the individuals feel better about themselves. In addition, in Teresa's case, had Sylvia been more forthcoming in her communications with Teresa after the layoff announcement was made, Teresa would have been less angry with Sylvia and the company, which would likely have staved off an expensive lawsuit for the company. Further, in the case of Zoe, early and frank supervisor communication would likely have avoided the negative effects on Zoe's morale, motivation, and productivity that the organization had to endure as a result of her supervisor's failure to properly communicate with her.

If a supervisor's bottom line is to motivate employees to be more productive, or to avoid getting employees unnecessarily angered or emotionally charged, communicating directly and effectively with them can have an important and positive effect on employees and can assist supervisors greatly in achieving those goals.

Know When to Back Off

Just as all persons at the workplace need to develop a sense for what battles to pick and when to pick them (see Chapter 5), supervisors and managers also need to know when to back off in their criticisms of their employees. If they pick every battle with their employees, or push their employees too far, they are likely to demoralize and demotivate them.

Consider the following example. Andrew is a real estate salesperson who works for Jennifer, the principal broker in a real estate office. Jennifer's office represented a seller in a real estate transaction and Andrew had been handling the sale on behalf of the office.

When the transaction was completed in principle, Andrew drafted the relevant paperwork and sent it to the buyer's broker by mail. Jennifer reviewed a copy of the paperwork later that day, after it was sent, but before it had been received by the other broker. During the course of her review of the relevant documents, Jennifer discovered that there was a minor mathematical error with respect to one of the dollar calculations in one of the documents, which needed to be corrected.

Jennifer then approached Andrew in a common area in the office, where a number of employees happened to be working. Rather than simply informing Andrew that there had been a mistake in the calculations and that the documents needed to be revised and sent again, Jennifer asked Andrew in front of all of his co-workers to explain how he arrived at the numbers that appeared in the documents.

At that moment, it became evident to Andrew that he had made an error. He immediately took several actions, all in Jennifer's presence and all in the presence of his colleagues and co-workers. First, he acknowledged that he made a mistake and apologized to Jennifer. He then directed his assistant to (1) insert the correct numbers into the document; (2) print out new originals of the document; (3) have them immediately messengered to the buyer's broker; and (4) call the appropriate people in the buyer's broker's office to inform them that the document they would be receiving by mail had a mistake in it and was corrected, and that the new document was being messengered over to them promptly. At that point, Andrew believed that the matter was resolved and proceeded to walk away from the area.

However, Jennifer insisted on continuing to discuss the issue and to harp on Andrew's mistake. She reiterated that it was unclear to her when she read the documents how he arrived at the numbers that he did.

Andrew responded by apologizing again for the oversight. He validated her apparent concerns by telling Jennifer that she was correct and that he had apparently made an inadvertent error in his calculations. He also indicated to Jennifer at that point that, as she had observed, the problem had been resolved. He reminded Jennifer that his assistant corrected the document; sent a new original to the buyer's broker by messenger; and called them to discard the first document and make use of the second one. Andrew was now fairly sure that the matter had been fully addressed and resolved, and once again proceeded to walk away from the area.

Jennifer, however, continued to rehash Andrew's mistake by once again stating that she could not figure out how he could have arrived at the numbers appearing in the original set of documents. Andrew, now somewhat perplexed, proceeded to explain the chronology of events yet again. Jennifer, still unsatisfied, proceeded to go over the mistake two more times before the two of them finally went their separate ways.

When Andrew returned to his work station, he was incredulous and quite irritated. He was also somewhat embarrassed, because this entire exchange had occurred in the common area in front of his assistant and several other employees.

He was completely demoralized by Jennifer's repeated comments. Although he had a number of additional projects that were pending for Jennifer at that time, the result of Jennifer's overzealous harping on Andrew's mistake was to make him unmotivated to work on any of those projects for the remainder of the day.

*   *   *

The point of the Jennifer/Andrew story is that supervisors and managers need to know when to back off, so that they do not cause their employees to become defensive, demoralized, unmotivated and, ultimately, less productive, which is in no one's best interests. Jennifer did not understand the effect that she was having on her employee and it cost her his productivity on other projects. Supervisors and managers need to understand that the more selective they are in their criticisms, the more positive and productive their employees are likely to be.

If You Must Criticize, Try to Be Positive and Constructive

Consider the following example, which involves two managers; two different management styles, strategies and approaches; and two different results in terms of effectiveness in motivating an employee.

Martin worked as an administrative assistant for Sandra and Jerome. Martin had some performance deficiencies which needed to be addressed and improved upon. Sandra and Jerome spoke with Martin about those deficiencies separately.

Sandra's approach was to focus exclusively on the negatives. She was extremely critical of Martin's weaknesses; did not discuss any of Martin's positive points; and offered no assistance or suggestions on how Martin could improve his performance. She was patronizing, antagonistic and even somewhat cruel in her approach with Martin. Martin interpreted Sandra's comments as an indication that she personally disliked him, although he did not understand and could not figure out why.

Sandra also wrote a very pointed memo summarizing all of Martin's weaknesses, which she placed in Martin's personnel file. She was more concerned about setting Martin up to fail and ultimately be fired than in trying to find a positive, creative solution to his performance problems. It was quite evident to Martin from his discussion with Sandra that she had no interest in assisting him in succeeding at his job.

By contrast, in Jerome's meeting with Martin, he identified Martin's negative points, but also extolled his strengths. In particular, Jerome went to great lengths in the meeting to reinforce a number of Martin's positive contributions to the overall work product and to the organization. He attempted to make Martin feel good about himself, while still providing constructive feedback on ways that he could and needed to improve.

Jerome prepared extensively for his discussion with Martin and gave considerable thought to (1) how to best motivate Martin; (2) how to make him feel good about himself; (3) how to engender loyalty from Martin; and (4) how to find ways for Martin to turn his negative issues around. Jerome sought to make a positive contribution toward Martin, both as a person and as an employee, and to make him believe that he could make a positive contribution to the organization.

Jerome provided Martin with examples of *how* to improve and examples on *why* things that he did incorrectly needed to be done in a different way. He gave Martin context. He made him feel like he was a part of the overall process, and a valued member of the organization. Jerome did not treat Martin like an underling. Rather, he tried to convince Martin that his contribution to the overall work product and to getting the job done were as important as Jerome's own contributions.

Jerome was validating, encouraging and patient in his approach. He gave Martin as much time as he could under the circumstances to show improvements and made himself available for follow-up questions so that Martin would be less likely repeat his mistakes over again.

* * *

Whom do you think Martin would be more motivated to try to please? As you might expect, Sandra's approach completely alienated Martin, while Jerome's approach motivated Martin to want to work harder both for Jerome and for the sake of the organization as a whole.

* * *

The lesson to be learned from the Sandra/Jerome/Martin scenario is that, if criticism is necessary by supervisors and managers, it will be much more effective, motivating, and well-received if it presented along with constructive, positive and reinforcing comments. Supervisors and managers should try to make employees feel like they are part of the team and that their work is necessary to achieve the overall goals of the organization.

It is also critically important for supervisors and managers to try to take the time to teach or train their employees. Explain *why* things need to be done in a certain manner or what the potential ramifications of a mistake might be.

In addition, supervisors and managers should also try to give examples whenever possible of suggested strategies for how individuals could improve and do things differently; and how they could better assist the organization in achieving its goals. It would also behoove supervisors and managers to find out what individuals' goals are and try to offer constructive suggestions for how they can achieve those goals. Finally, it might also be helpful to try to explain how the employee's work fits in to the overall organization goals (the overall puzzle) and why that work is significant.

In short, the more that supervisors and managers validate and positively reinforce their employees, and the more those individuals believe that they are a part of their organizations, the more motivated and productive they are likely to be.

CHAPTER 8

A Message for Non-Managers: Understanding What Drives Your Supervisors and Managers

This Chapter is directed specifically at non-managers. Unfortunately, sometimes non-managers unnecessarily develop negative attitudes about their supervisors and/or unnecessarily complain about the specific working conditions that their supervisors may create. Commonly, the reason for those negative attitudes is that non-managers tend to view their own specific jobs in a vacuum, without really understanding what their supervisors and managers do all day or what the breadth of their supervisors' responsibilities are.

The purpose of this Chapter is to educate non-managers about some of the issues that their supervisors and managers deal with on a daily basis. The underlying premise is that, if non-managers can develop a better understanding of their supervisors, they might be (1) less negative about how they believe that they are being treated at work; (2) less likely to complain to or about their supervisors about working conditions (or, if they do complain, more likely to do so selectively and at appropriate times); (3) more likely to try to work effectively *with* (rather than against) their supervisors; and (4) more likely to be able to put their own work experiences into their proper perspective. By developing a better understanding of their supervisors, non-managers will hopefully be able to develop strategies for working more productively with their bosses, thereby making their own overall work experiences more positive and pleasant.

Common Misconceptions about Supervisors and Managers

There are a number of misconceptions that non-managers commonly have about their supervisors and managers. Non-managers need to be sensitive to these issues and try to dispel these myths in order to work more effectively with their bosses.

For example, non-managers often have an image of their supervisors and managers as the "proverbial" bosses who sit in their offices with their feet on their desks, smoking cigars and counting their money. However, what non-managers need to understand is that there is a *reason* why those individuals are supervisors, managers, bosses, and/or owners of businesses. They typically are smart. They typically are decision-makers. They more often than not are risk takers. They usually are (or at least to achieve their current status were) very hard working. They frequently are busy people whose time is at a premium and whose time should not be wasted.

In addition, there is also a common misconception among non-managers that supervisors are always thinking of their employees and *nothing but* their employees. In reality, however, managers have enormous responsibilities and pressures, many of which compete with each other; need to be balanced against each other on a daily basis; need to be prioritized; need to be addressed simultaneously; and/or are fairly complex.

Finally, non-managers also need to understand that supervisors frequently need to react on a very quick turnaround time to a broad range of issues which can impact on *all* employees in their charge, not just on one individual. What this means is that supervisors and managers typically do not have the luxury of evaluating a discreet issue based *only* on how it might personally affect *one* individual, even if that one individual might happen to be negatively affected by a particular decision.

Supervisors Are People, Too

It is also common for employees to think of or refer to the organizations for which they work in terms of amorphous, intangible entities such as, for example, the "Firm," the "Company," the "Organization," the "Agency," or the "Department." When this happens, individuals can sometimes lose sight of the fact that the mysterious "entity" for which they work is actually made up of real live people with their own individual problems and agendas.

The fact is that organizations are run by managers who are human beings with mortgages, families, kids, spouses, and responsibilities, just like non-managers. In their efforts to better understand and get along with their supervisors, it is important for non-managers to remember that supervisors and managers can have bad days and personal problems, too.

One way for non-managers to make their work experiences more positive is to lose the "us against them" attitude toward supervisors and managers and remind themselves that "management" is in fact made up of individuals. Non-managers are far more likely to get what they want from their managers and their workplace situations generally if they take an interest in (1) recognizing that their supervisors are people, too; and (2) learning what those supervisors as people might be going through themselves.

Common Supervisor Responsibilities

Many non-managers are not aware on a basic level of what

occupies their supervisors' and managers' time or of the various competing interests that those individuals often have to contend with. Before non-managers complain that they are being mistreated, they should at least understand what their supervisors go through on a daily basis. Before they complain that their supervisors have too many "perks," they should at least develop a better understanding of the responsibilities that go along with those "perks."

Consider the following example. Barbara works as a receptionist for Steve, who owns his own general construction contracting business. Steve employs six or seven people to work in the company's main office. In addition, another ten people are employed by the company on salary in the field. Steve's contracting business hires subcontracting companies to perform some of the actual construction work on a job-by-job basis.

In years past, typically at the end of the calendar year, Steve gave his employees annual raises and bonuses, which historically were based on the profitability of the business during that calendar year. One year, Steve called all of the employees together to inform them that, because of a slowdown in the economy which had an enormous effect on the construction industry in particular, the company had had a very poor year financially and could not afford to give anyone raises or bonuses for that year. Steve's employees were disappointed to hear that news.

Barbara was particularly vocal about her objections. She told several of the employees that she did not believe that Steve was telling the truth about the financial state of the company. As proof, she reminded her co-workers that, despite the apparent economic crisis that the company was facing, Steve somehow managed to scrape up enough money to take his family to Hawaii for the holidays, as he had in years past.

Barbara caused a great stir in the office and contributed greatly and unnecessarily to the low morale among employees. She clearly did not understand Steve's "big picture." She did not distinguish between Steve's personal assets and the assets of the business. She did not understand that, just because Steve could afford to take even a $10,000 personal vacation, his business payroll could nevertheless not necessarily afford the additional expense of raises and bonuses, which in prior years sometimes exceeded *$200,000*.

What Barbara did not know was that Steve has owned his business for 35 years and has built a large personal nestegg, out of which, among other things, he pays for the college education for his four children; invests in retirement accounts; and pays for annual vacations for his family. Not that Steve owes Barbara or any of his employees an explanation for taking a vacation. He has enormous responsibilities as the owner of his business and an employer of approximately 20 people. He has earned the right to enjoy his personal wealth, regardless of what his employees might think.

*   *   *

The Barbara/Steve scenario is a classic example of a non-manager not necessarily understanding her boss' "big picture." The lesson to be learned here is that non-managers *should* understand more about a supervisor's "big picture," including all of his or her obligations and responsibilities, before jumping on the "I-have-been-mistreated" or the "I-am-entitled-to-certain-benefits-from-my-employer" bandwagons. Non-managers need to understand that supervisors and managers have many competing interests, responsibilities, obligations and job duties, all of which the non-managers may not necessarily be privy to.

*   *   *

What follows are examples of common responsibilities that many supervisors in a variety of types of organizations may have. These responsibilities tend to be overlooked by non-managers when they complain about being mistreated or of excessive supervisor "perks." (Remember, the goal here is to create a better understanding of supervisor responsibilities, so that non-managers can work more effectively *with* their managers.)

The Bottom Line

Supervisors and managers in many organizations are concerned about the organization's "bottom line." The bottom line in the private sector is to make sure that the organization is profitable. In addition, in all work sectors (public, nonprofit and private), supervisors' and managers' bottom lines are also to ensure that employees and the organizations as a whole are productive; are within budget; and are appropriately moving toward achieving their goals.

Constituents

Supervisors and managers in most organizations have bosses and/ or other "constituents" to whom they are answerable, such as clients, customers, and/or board members. They have to perform their *own* jobs at certain levels in order to keep those jobs. Constituents can be very demanding. Supervisors and managers must make sure that the people that they "report to" are serviced and that their demands are satisfied on a regular basis.

Meeting Expenses and Payroll

Supervisors and managers also can be responsible for making sure that all bills of the organization are paid and that payroll expenses are satisfied. This involves not only (1) making sure that sufficient income is coming into the organization to meet bills, expenses and payroll, but also (2) supervising other employees to make sure that all of those expenses are being paid properly and timely to the appropriate persons.

Rainmaking

Supervisors and managers sometimes are directly responsible for "rainmaking," or generating additional income for the organization. It is a competitive world. In order to keep organizations liquid and running, many supervisors and managers need to make sure that not only are existing clients being serviced properly and in a timely manner, but also that new customers and clients, who can produce additional revenues, are constantly being cultivated.

Employee Relations

Supervisors and managers also need to be mindful on a daily basis of numerous employee relations issues relating to employees in their charge. They are commonly responsible for monitoring and evaluating the performance of all of their employees. Sometimes, petty squabbles between employees need to be mediated, managed and/or resolved by supervisors. Sometimes, serious employee relations complaints, such as complaints of sexual harassment, which the employer may be legally required to promptly investigate, address, and remedy if necessary and appropriate, need to be dealt with by supervisors as well.

Business (or Organizational) Administration

Depending on the type of organization and the number of employees that a given organization has, supervisors and managers commonly can make dozens of decisions on a daily, weekly or monthly basis relating to the administration of the organization generally, such as decisions relating to financial planning, business equipment planning, updating computer systems, updating copying systems, updating fax and phone systems, and revising office management systems generally.

*   *   *

In short, it is imperative that, before employees jump on the "mistreatment" or "entitlements" bandwagons, they should understand what supervisors go through and what their responsibilities are. The more tuned in to supervisors' responsibilities that non-managers are, (1) the more they will understand their supervisors and what motivates them; (2) the better able they will be to get what they want from those supervisors: and (3) the better able they will be to make their work environment more positive.

Supervisor Agendas

Non-managers not only need to know what their supervisors and managers *do* all day long, but they also need to know also *why* their supervisors and managers engage in the behaviors that they do. The "why" question can often be answered by developing an understanding of common supervisor agendas. Once non-managers understand what *motivates* their supervisors and managers to act the way they do, they might be better able to develop strategies for working successfully with them.

Some common supervisor agendas consistent with common organizational goals and supervisory responsibilities include making money for themselves and for their organizations; getting their work, and the work of their employees, done productively, efficiently and without complaint; and pleasing constituents. These are fairly straightforward and are addressed in the prior section.

Other common supervisor agendas that perhaps are more personally driven include (1) maintaining power and control over others; and/or (2) having one's ego stroked. These kinds of agendas are not as easily recognizable and provide more of a challenge for the non-manager in attempting to develop strategies to successfully work with individuals who may have these agendas.

Consider the following example. Richard, a senior manager at one company, is having a personal relationship with Nadine, a mid-level manager at a competitor company in the same local area. Jay initially worked for Nadine's company. He worked with Nadine on a few isolated projects over a period of two years, but did not get along with her.

Eventually, Jay sought out new employment and was hired by Richard's organization. Richard did not interview Jay prior to his hire and Jay had no reason to mention during the interview process that he had occasionally worked with Nadine while employed at the competitor company.

When Jay left Nadine's employ, she was unaware that he went to work for Richard's company. Nor did Richard know when his company hired Jay that Jay had previously worked directly with Nadine on any project or that they did not get along.

Once Jay started working for his new employer, however, he did hear casual references to the fact that Richard knew or perhaps was even romantically involved with Nadine. At the times that he heard those comments, he did not see the relevance of them to his employment situation and did not pay much attention to them.

Several months passed after Jay became employed with Richard's organization without incident. Then one day, Jay was scheduled to give a presentation to Richard and other senior managers at his new company. Richard happened to mention to Nadine during a telephone conversation that Jay, the company's new "rising star," was giving a presentation that day. Learning for the first time that Jay was now working at Richard's company, and still bitter over some disagreements that she had had with Jay, Nadine proceeded to badmouth Jay to Richard.

Richard, learning that Jay had somehow previously offended his "girlfriend," decided that he would use the senior management meeting as an opportunity to "punish" Jay for what Nadine claimed that Jay had done to her. Richard heckled and humiliated Jay during his presentation, a level of embarrassment from which Jay would not be able to easily recover in the eyes of a number of senior managers in the organization for months to come.

*   *   *

There were several personally-motivated agendas at work in the Richard/Nadine/Jay scenario. Nadine was being somewhat petty and vindictive, reaching her hand up from the proverbial "grave" in an effort to damage Jay's reputation and perhaps even stunt his career growth. She knew that telling Richard some bad things about Jay would motivate Richard to take some negative action against Jay.

In addition, Richard himself had an agenda. His agenda was to show Jay who was boss and to wield power and authority over him simply because he *could*. (Unfortunately, this kind of agenda is perhaps too common among supervisors in many organizations.)

* * *

Further, how many of us in our workplaces over the years have experienced the supervisor who *purports* to be every employee's friend, but in reality just wants to have his ego stroked and to maintain as much control over non-managers as he possibly can as often as he possibly can? **Consider the following example.**

Kevin is a supervisor. He manages a number of people, including Curtis. Kevin routinely invites Curtis and his family over to his house for holiday celebrations during the course of the year. Curtis, though uncomfortable with attending those functions, frequently does so because his boss has invited him and because he is afraid to reject any such invitation, for fear of reprisal by Kevin at work.

In one such instance, Curtis and his family happened to have made alternative plans and he was unable to attend a holiday celebration at Kevin's home. He made no mention of the prearranged plans to Kevin. At the last minute, on the Friday before the long holiday weekend, Kevin extended an invitation to Curtis. Curtis declined the invitation, stating only that he and his family had "made other plans."

Even though Curtis had a legitimate reason for declining the invitation, Kevin was not made aware of what that specific reason was. Under the circumstances, Kevin did not understand how Curtis could possibly not attend his party, thinking that the gesture of even inviting Curtis was quite magnanimous. Kevin became personally insulted; did not believe that Curtis was telling the truth about being unable to attend; and concluded that Curtis simply did not want to socialize with Kevin and his family. (Remember the "Eye-of-the-Beholder Syndrome" described in the previous Chapter?)

Upon hearing that Curtis could not attend his party, Kevin became angered and all of a sudden reverted back to being "the boss." In the same conversation in which Curtis indicated that he could not attend Kevin's holiday function during the upcoming weekend, Kevin informed Curtis for the first time that a deadline for the project that they had been working on had been moved up. He instructed Curtis that the finished product needed to be reviewed by Kevin first thing Tuesday morning, knowing full well that Curtis would have to work most of the holiday weekend, and perhaps even rearrange his previously scheduled holiday plans, in order to get the project done by the new deadline.

*   *   *

The Kevin/Curtis scenario provides another illustration of a supervisor wielding power and authority over an employee simply because he *can*. Kevin wanted his ego stroked and when Curtis did not stroke it, Kevin then used his power to exact a form of personal revenge.

*   *   *

Could Jay and Curtis have avoided the wrath of their supervisors in the scenarios described above? Perhaps if they knew and understood their supervisors' agendas, they might have been able to anticipate the kinds of problems they might face from their supervisors and figure out in advance of those problems actually occurring how to best respond to them.

For example, in the Jay scenario, had Jay paid more attention to casual conversations in the office involving Richard and Nadine, it might have occurred to him that they were involved in a relationship. Certainly, once he realized that that was a possibility, it may have dawned on him that Nadine might badmouth him to Richard; that Richard might believe her; and that Richard might even try to sabotage Jay at some point.

A prudent strategy for Jay at that point might have been to engage in a "preemptive strike" of his own, by casually mentioning Nadine and some of the problems that he had with her in his prior job (and thereby putting his own "spin" on those issues) to some of the other senior managers at his new company. That way, Jay could have at least laid the groundwork to protect himself in the event that Richard *did* try to sabotage him, giving himself a fighting chance when Richard attacked that some of the other senior managers who knew about the Richard/Nadine relationship might question Richard's credibility and/or motivation for doing so.

Similarly, in the Curtis scenario, perhaps he could have avoided Kevin's wrath by anticipating Kevin's invitation and casually mentioning his plans to Kevin in passing in *advance* of receiving the invitation, thereby "preempting" the awkwardness of actually receiving the invitation. In addition, to the extent that Curtis was aware that Kevin's ego was so large that he had a propensity to be personally insulted by anyone who did not respond favorably to his so-called "magnanimous" gestures, perhaps Curtis could have provided his boss with more details about his plans, thereby preempting the possibility that Kevin would convince himself that Curtis was not telling the truth about having plans.

* * *

The bottom line here is that, if non-managers have better understandings of what motivates their supervisors and learn to recognize what their supervisors' agendas might be, they might be able to anticipate these kinds of scenarios and act accordingly to preempt them from happening over and over or from occurring at all.

Politics Between Managers

In order to fully understand the work experiences of supervisors and managers, non-managers must also understand the relationships that managers have with *each other*. Each supervisor typically has his or her own dynamic with every other supervisor in his or her organization. Those dynamics often shape and influence how each supervisor acts or treats others at work.

Sometimes, for example, supervisors have agendas vis-à-vis each other. Sometimes, there are power struggles between supervisors, or between managers, based upon who generates more revenues for the organization. Sometimes, supervisors and managers are competitive with each other, perhaps vying for the same promotion or for the same boss' ear. Sometimes, managers do not even like or respect each other. Sometimes, managers simply try to get along with other managers because it is expedient to do so. Sometimes, managers need each other because each has his or her strengths and the skills of each are necessary for the success of the organization as a whole.

What follows is a discussion of various types of managers and manager relationships that non-managers are likely to encounter at the workplace, as well as some suggested strategies for dealing with those situations and relationships as they arise.

Manager Factions

From time to time, everyone in the workplace experiences "factions" among managers. This occurs when certain managers in an organization align themselves with other managers and/or employees, while other managers who are in competition with the first group align themselves with still other managers or employees. Delicate political problems can develop among non-managers in these situations, who may be forced to make a choice to align themselves with one camp or the other.

Consider the following example. Tanya and Jessica are mid-level managers at the same level in their organization. Both report directly to Dorothy, who is a Vice President. Both work in the same general area of the company. Although Tanya and Jessica technically supervise different individuals; technically work in different departments; and technically are responsible for different organizational functions, there is some overlap between their employees and their respective functions.

Tanya and Jessica are very competitive with each other and are threatened by each other. There is one opening for a director-level position for which each is qualified and into which each desperately wants to be promoted. Both Tanya and Jessica are trying to "court" and perhaps influence Dorothy, who will be making the promotion decision, and both are badmouthing the other in order to get a leg up in the promotion process.

In their efforts to make themselves look good and make the other look bad, both Tanya and Jessica are building coalitions of support from the various employees in their respective departments. Non-management employees are put in the position of having to choose which faction to be a part of. Some employees believe that they are being "forced" to choose only one side. They fear retribution from the side that they do not choose.

*   *   *

What should non-managers do when faced with this type of situation? There are several possibilities, all of which are related to each other. First, try to avoid alienating any group or faction as a whole or, at a minimum, any particularly influential persons within any given faction. One never knows which individuals might be important for the non-managers themselves to cultivate as allies in order to maximize *their own* abilities to get what *they* want from their *own* work experiences.

Second, non-managers should also try not to align themselves *exclusively* with one faction. Try to keep a toe in the water of both camps to avoid alienating *anyone*, if possible.

Third, try to straddle the fence between the factions wherever possible. Try not to take a position which is openly in support of one faction and/or openly against the other. This could involve (1) not jumping on anyone's bandwagon; (2) gaining the confidences of managers and non-managers alike from all factions; (3) holding and protecting those confidences; and (4) not "snitching" to one faction about the confidences that may have been obtained from the other camp.

Fourth, try not to badmouth members of one faction to members of the other. The quickest way to find yourself in a political mess is to badmouth one faction to another or reveal confidences between warring factions.

Finally, if you *do* happen to find yourself in a position where you are unwittingly being placed in the middle of two competing factions at work, try to pick an appropriate moment to make it known that you are uncomfortable with being put in the middle. The goal is to encourage the power players in each faction to work out their differences with each other and not through you. (Be delicate in your approach, however. Being too aggressive in this regard might inadvertently and unnecessarily alienate some players that you would like to have in your own camp.)

The "Kiss-and-Make-Up Syndrome"

Another political scenario between managers is the "kiss-and-make-up" scenario. Remember, managers can have complex relationships with each other that non-managers are not always entirely aware of and/or do not always entirely understand. What often happens when non-managers find themselves in the middle of a political struggle between two managers is that the two managers eventually (and figuratively) "kiss and make up," and then use the employee who got caught in the middle (and who has now fallen victim to the "kiss-and-make-up syndrome") as a scapegoat for present or future problems which arise.

Consider the following example as an illustration of what sometimes happens to non-managers who find themselves caught up in a battle between two "dueling" managers. Lawrence is a non-manager who works for both Kelly and Regina. Unbeknownst to Lawrence, Kelly and Regina have unresolved political issues between them. Lawrence complains to Kelly about Regina. Kelly uses that information to discredit and embarrass Regina at a management meeting. Regina now views Lawrence as an enemy.

Later on, and also unbeknownst to Lawrence, Kelly and Regina decide to patch things up between themselves because they realize that their personal, political battle is not in the best interests of the organization as a whole. Kelly and Regina have done the proverbial "kiss-and-make-up" and have now decided that their interests are more aligned than they previously had thought.

However, Lawrence has already alienated Regina and she is not inclined to forgive him. At the appropriate time, Regina will attempt to use Lawrence as a scapegoat for a negative issue that arises. She lobbies the management group to terminate or discipline Lawrence. Kelly, now an ally of Regina's based upon what she believes to be the greater good of the organization, does not protect Lawrence, who is left hanging out to dry.

*   *   *

This scenario occurs more often than people might think. One way to avoid getting caught in the middle of "dueling managers" scenario is to stay out of the political fray and just continue to "do the work." Listen when the managers may complain to you about each other, but try to avoid taking sides.

In addition, certainly try to avoid complaining to one about the other, unless you are confident that doing so is not likely to bite you in the back if they should happen to "kiss and make up."

All Managers Are Not Created Equal

Another important point to remember when trying to develop an understanding of supervisors and managers is that not all managers are created equal. There are different levels of management within each organization and different levels of power and influence among managers.

In fact, even with respect to supervisors or managers who are technically at the same level in a given organization, there still can be different levels of political clout and power that they can have *within* that organization. Those differences can be based, for example, upon business or revenue generation; workload; skills; or degree of influence on more senior power players in the organization.

In this regard, non-managers need to be able to recognize who is who. They need to learn to distinguish between the true power players at all levels of management and those managers with less power and influence at each level. Making those distinctions will enable non-managers to plan more effective strategies for successfully working with all management-level employees. What follows are some ways to identify managers with various degrees of power and some strategies for effectively dealing with each.

Power Players

The power players are the ones who will have the most influence over (1) workload assignments; (2) workload distribution; and (3) determinations about whom non-managers will likely work with. Obviously, all employees need to be sensitive to the needs of power players and do whatever is necessary to get into their camps. Few people can succeed in getting what they want from any organization without the support of the power players.

Non-Power Players

There are three principal types of non-power managers in many workplaces: the "powerless mid-level managers"; the "clone" managers; and the "power-hungry mid-level managers." Descriptions and strategies for working effectively with each are set forth below.

"Powerless Mid-Level Managers"

The "powerless mid-level managers" typically have very little power and influence in many areas of organizational politics. These individuals mean well, but are afraid of their own shadows. They rarely go out on a limb for their employees or even for themselves. They work hard; are comfortable in their positions in the overall organizational hierarchy; and accept their power limits.

The key strategies for working successfully with these individuals are to (1) try to impress them; and (2) try not to underestimate them. Just because they may have limited power or influence in some areas does not mean that they have *no* power or influence in *any* area. Whatever limited power or influence they *do* have is derived from the fact that they work hard and are respected for working hard. Because their opinions with respect to the work itself can sometimes be valued by the power players, failing to impress them may cause them to complain, which in turn could create a negative situation for the unsuspecting non-manager.

On the other hand, impressing the "powerless mid-level managers" does not necessarily translate into increasing the positives of an employee's overall work experience because these individuals usually have limited desire or ability to actually *assist* employees in getting what they want. These types of managers typically do not stick their necks out for anyone. Further, although they sometimes *do* have the ability to leave power players with negative impressions of others, they often have little ability to influence the power players positively or in someone's favor.

In short, the "powerless mid-level managers" often have the power to *hurt* you, but very little power to *help* you. The best that you can hope for in working with these individuals is that you impress them enough so that you can neutralize them to avoid having them *negatively* impact on your work situation.

"Clone" Managers

The second group of non-power managers are the "clone" managers, whom we have all encountered from time to time. "Clone" managers are told what to think by the power players in their organizations and they believe what they are told. They rarely think for themselves with respect to any management issue. They understand the image that the organization would like its managers to have and almost robotically try to conform to that image. They tend to think and act like all other managers in the organization, or at least in the manner they believe all managers are *supposed* to think and act in that organization.

"Clone" managers are also the consummate team players. They will sacrifice themselves for the good of the organization.

Strategies for working with "clone" managers are similar to those used for working with the "powerless mid-level managers." *Do* the work. *Develop* these individuals as allies. Do *not* rely on them to assist you in getting what you want. For that, focus on developing relationships with the power players in the organization.

"Power-Hungry Mid-Level Managers"

The third group of non-power managers are the "power-hungry mid-level managers" (a group which sometimes also includes the "ambitious boot lickers"). These are individuals who do not actually have as much power as they think they do or would like to have. They desperately and relentlessly work on developing a larger power base and tend to do whatever is necessary to acquire that power. In addition, these individuals also seem to commonly have the ear of one or more of the senior managers or power players in the organization.

Be wary of these individuals. If they feel threatened, they can turn on you and use their influence with the power players to hurt you.

Try to avoid working with them if possible. However, if you must work with them, do the work and try to impress them. In addition, try to do what you can to lead them to believe that you support them and are in their camp. They will be less likely to badmouth you if they do not view you as a threat.

Further, try to avoid putting yourself in situations in which these types of managers speak for you or plead your case. Rather, try to make sure that you talk yourself up and politick directly with all power players in the organization, particularly those who might be influenced by the "power-hungry" individuals.

It is dangerous to rely on the "power-hungry mid-level managers" even to say anything positive about you to any of the power players in the organization. Chances are that, if something positive happens, these individuals will try to take the credit. On the other hand, if something negative happens (regardless of whose fault it might be), these individuals are certainly capable of blaming you or other non-management employees for those negative results.

For these reasons, it is imperative when working with these individuals to make sure that you get proper credit for the positive things that you do and that you minimize the potential negatives by making sure that you get to put your own "spin" on those events. One key for non-managers to enjoy successful working relationships with "power-hungry mid-level managers" is not to give them too much control over *your* destiny and, to the fullest extent that *you* possibly can, maintain control over the content of information, positive or negative, that the power players receive about *you.*

Understanding the "Chain-of-Yelling Principle"

The "chain-of-yelling principle" refers to the inevitable chain of accountability which exists in all organizations (although hopefully in practice it is more of an *accountability* issue than an actual *yelling* issue). The way it works is as follows.

Everyone in the workplace either has a direct boss or is indirectly accountable to *someone else* for the consequences of his or her actions. For example, non-managers are typically accountable to their supervisors and managers. Supervisors and mid-level managers are typically accountable to senior managers and sometimes directly to clients, customers or other constituents of the organization. Senior managers are typically also accountable to clients and customers, as well as to officers, directors, and board members of the organization. In turn, those individuals are typically accountable to shareholders (if the organization is a publicly held); family members (if privately held); and/or sometimes governmental agencies or other members of the public.

Non-managers need to understand the "chain-of-yelling" in their own organizations in order to truly understand the relationships that their supervisors and managers have with those people to whom *they* are directly accountable; and the attendant pressures, stresses and responsibilities that their supervisors may have as a result of those relationships.

Consider the following example as an illustration of how the "chain-of-yelling" principle can work in practice. Charlotte is a member of the Board of Directors of a medium-sized company. She is unsatisfied with a particular action that was taken by the company and/or authorized by a senior management person. The Board discusses the issue and it is decided that Charlotte needs to speak with Jane, the CEO of the company, about the problem.

Jane, who was not involved in the specifics of the action

taken, then proceeds to chastise several of her senior managers in response to Charlotte's criticisms. Each of those senior managers then proceeds to chastise the middle managers under *their* charge. In turn, the middle managers then proceed to chastise various employees in *their* charge.

To complicate the example further and demonstrate the potential breadth of the "chain-of-yelling" principle, imagine further that senior management of the company has formed a belief that the current unsatisfactory situation is a result of advice given or research done by the company's lawyers. In that instance, Jane, the CEO, or certain of her designated senior managers, in addition to chastising their own employees, might also chastise the senior lawyers at the law firm which provided the questionable advice. The senior lawyers at the firm might in turn chastise the junior lawyers who actually worked on the project, who, in turn, might chastise their own support staff members.

* * *

At the end of this particular chain is Melissa, an assistant to one of the junior lawyers at the law firm, who, on a very personal level, believes that she has been treated unfairly by her direct boss. All that the unsuspecting Melissa (and perhaps other non-managers like her throughout the chain) knows is that her boss is unhappy with her. This can obviously have a debilitating effect on her morale and productivity, particularly if she believes that she did nothing wrong.

One strategy for Melissa (and others like her) is to discuss the issue directly with her boss. She needs to tell her boss how his actions made her feel. In addition, by talking it out, hopefully Melissa (and others like her) can develop a better understanding of the entire "chain-of-yelling" in the organization (or at least the chain that caused this particular problem).

* * *

More generally, non-managers should take note from the Jane-to-Melissa scenario of how many people can be (and were) affected by one board member's dissatisfaction. Given how long the chain can be and how many people can be directly or indirectly impacted by the chain, it is easy to see why developing a better understanding of the entire "chain-of-yelling" can only help non-managers to work more productively, positively and effectively with their managers.

Specifically, if non-managers understood the "chain-of-yelling" in their organizations, perhaps they might better understand the pressures that their bosses are under. To the extent that they understand that the "yelling" had more to do with their own boss' frustrations than their actual work performance, perhaps their morale and productivity would not be as low.

In addition, although "yelling" at an assistant (or at anyone at any level) is certainly not to be condoned, and typically is not particularly productive or motivating, if non-managers understood the "chain-of-yelling," perhaps they could also effectively build a tolerance for their supervisors' behaviors (assuming of course that it is occasional rather than regular).

Finally, if non-managers understood the "chain-of-yelling," perhaps they could learn to anticipate the types of problems that tend to cause the chain to occur in the first place and attempt to resolve those problems within their or their boss' control in *advance* of them actually occurring (thereby perhaps eliminating the need for the chain itself or for the actual yelling.) In those circumstances, non-managers might even be able to figure out ways in which they could better assist their bosses from making the same kind of mistakes over and over again.

* * *

In summary, it is in the best interests of everyone in an organization that non-managers develop a better understanding of their supervisors and managers. The better employees understand what their supervisors think; what their supervisors' responsibilities are; and why their supervisors act the way they do, the more likely that non-managers, their bosses and hopefully everyone in their organizations will be able to effectively make their collective work experiences more positive, productive and pleasant.

CHAPTER 9

Outside and Other Influences

This Chapter addresses political issues that may arise with persons with whom you do not necessarily work directly, but who nevertheless sometimes have the ability to impact on your work situation. The purpose here is to provide strategies for dealing with family members on the home front, and/or third parties whom you might need to interact with on the work front, such as clients, customers, competitors, and other contractors with whom your organization does business, so that their influences can help, rather than hinder, your efforts to make your overall work experience more positive.

Family Politics

A critical component in making your work life more positive and productive is how you deal with work-related issues at home. **Ask yourself the following questions.** Do you bring work-related issues home with you? To what degree? Do you actually physically bring work home with you to complete? How often? Do you remain stressed out after the workday ends? To what extent do you relive your entire workday with your spouse, children, family members, partner, roommate, loved ones or friends after work? If your answers to any of these questions suggest that you might be blurring the line between work life and home life, you may need to work on creating a balance between the two. The following scenarios (1) identify some common problems that individuals face in bringing too much of their work life home with them; and (2) offer some insights into possible strategies to employ at home to create an appropriate balance between home and work life, and ultimately reduce stress levels both at home and at work.

"Living and Retelling"

Some people believe that half of life is "living" and the other half is "retelling" stories about what happened while "living." In the abstract, "living and retelling" can be an interesting and life-affirming philosophy.

However, when the "living" component involves work and the "retelling" component involves coming home and sharing everything that happens at work with friends, family members, and/or others who might share your household or be personally close to you, sometimes this philosophy is not always the best strategy to employ, particularly if your work life is, or workdays are, particularly stressful or unpleasant.

Consider the following example. William and Gina are married. They have no children. Both have responsible positions in their respective fields and both of their jobs are fairly high-stress.

They are both animated people who are passionate about their work. Every night, they look forward to seeing each other and telling each other every detail about their respective work days. Each is intimately familiar with all of the principal players at the other's workplace. It is not uncommon for one or both of them to burst onto the scene at home and recount all of the significant stories or events which occurred during their workdays, particularly some of the more stressful and/or political issues. Generally, one of them tells all of his or her stories within minutes of first greeting the other at the end of the workday; then the other tells all of his or her stories for the day over dinner.

Not surprisingly, these conversations tend to be very high-energy. Sometimes, however, the result of these conversations is that the person who is retelling all of his or her stories to the other is also reliving the events and the stress of those events.

For William and Gina, reliving negative work-related stories at home can sometimes manifest itself physically. William, for example, might occasionally feel palpitations; have pains in his stomach; or have difficulty digesting when retelling one of his particularly painful work-related stories to Gina. Gina, on the other hand, tends to become very hyper and nervous, and sometimes has difficulty breathing, when retelling her own stories to William.

*   *   *

The concern about the William/Gina dynamic is that it can actually add to, rather than reduce, one's overall stress level, both at home and, ultimately, at work. Because both William and Gina (and perhaps others like them) are very emotional and animated, they need to be careful to ensure that their exchanges do not have the exact opposite effect from the desired one. They need to make sure that, rather than "freaking each other into a frenzy," they try to perpetuate a relaxing home environment for themselves.

At a minimum, a likely result from such "retelling" is that it makes for a not-so-relaxing evening, series of evenings, or lifestyle. Sometimes, after a "retelling" session, it can take William, Gina or others like them several hours to decompress, assuming that that can be accomplished at all. What this means is that the individuals doing the "retelling" might either be stressed out when they go to sleep or stay up later than necessary to effectively relax.

Going to sleep late, even though they will still have to get up early (or at the same time as usual) the following day, may result in their being tired, less productive and/or irritable at work, which will of course increase their overall stress levels and tend to make work experiences under those circumstances less positive.

Once on this vicious cycle, it may last all week and perhaps not correct itself until the following weekend. In fact, if these individuals are not careful, this pattern can even continue for weeks or months.

*   *   *

For these reasons, sometimes it may be necessary to rethink the "living and retelling" strategy, or at least the degree to which you are willing to "live and retell," as it relates to bringing work-related issues home with you.

"Kicking the Dog"

The "Kicking-the-Dog Syndrome" is a sometimes unpleasant, logical extension of the "Chain-of-Yelling Principle," which was discussed in the prior Chapter. In the work-related "Chain-of-Yelling," a manager of an organization is "yelled" at by an owner or customer of the organization. The manager then "yells" at a subordinate, who in turn "yells" at another subordinate.

The "Kicking-the-Dog Syndrome" involves persons in the "chain" coming home after long, tiring, stressful days at work in which they feel as if *they* were beaten up (figuratively) or "yelled" at, and taking out the stresses of those days on *their* spouses, children, parents, family members, loved ones, partners, roommates, or the proverbial (or actual) dog or family pet.

It is important to make every effort *not* to "kick the proverbial dog" when you get home from work. It is not positive, productive or useful to take your workplace or workday stresses out on family members by "yelling" at someone at home. Remember, no matter how hard your workday was; who "yelled" at you; or what you may have done wrong, it is typically not the fault of anyone in your family.

In fact, quite the contrary is true. Family members are often your biggest supporters. These are the people who can provide critical positive reinforcement that working people need in order to get up every day and *face* the rigors of work.

Most people *need* the support of family members and loved ones to get *through* the rough times at work. Without that support, the rough times at work may be even *more* difficult to deal with.

The last thing you want to do is "kick the dog" and *alienate* the very people who are typically at the core of your support system. Doing so is likely to *increase*, rather than decrease, your stress levels both at home and, ultimately, through the "spill-over effect," at work. (Of course, the more stress and negativity you bring to work from home, the less positive your overall work experience is likely to be.)

Understanding the Limitations of Family Advice

Sometimes, people also need to be aware that spouses, family members and loved ones may not always be the best persons to provide advice with respect to stressful work situations, despite their best intentions. On the positive side, family members and loved ones often can provide unconditional loyalty. They sometimes feel what you feel and can be very supportive.

On the negative side, however, sometimes their desire to protect you from being hurt at all costs makes them less than totally objective. For example, loyal family members sometimes are capable of unwittingly "jumping on the bandwagon," and being hyper-critical of anyone at your workplace whom they perceive is not treating you well enough. When this occurs, loved ones' emotions may end up making you *more* stressed out than you might have been if you had *not* filled them in on what happened at work, or solicited their advice about the work-related problem.

Under these circumstances, you may need to "filter" the remarks of those loved ones and/or the positions that they encourage you to take. You may also need to encourage loved ones just to *listen* and *not* add fuel to the proverbial fire.

Finally, it is often important under these circumstances to try to avoid *following* loved ones blindly and/or *jumping* on their work-related bandwagons, particularly when your instincts (or trusted colleagues) tell you *not* to. Remember that, at the "end of the day," *you* are the one who needs to deal directly with the issues that arise at *your* workplace. Be careful not to let your family members' emotions, support, and/or loyalty *taint* your view (or a more objective view) of what needs to be done, or what strategies need to be employed, at work in order to maximize *your* chances to make *your* work experience more positive and productive.

Bringing Work Home with You

Many people bring work home with them in some form, whether it be mentally, emotionally, or actually physically bringing home work to be done at night or on a weekend. Sometimes, people's jobs demand that they do so.

A very simple, common sense word to the wise is appropriate here. Try very hard not to bring work home, if and when it is at all possible. Depending on the type of job that you have and the extent of your responsibilities in that job, that might be easier said than done.

However, remember that everyone needs down time. Everyone needs to relax. Sometimes, people forget that they need those things. People *need* to spend time doing whatever it is that they enjoy doing when they are not working. Even thinking about work at home can distract you from your spouse, kids, family, house, garden, hobbies and other personal activities. You will not be your most productive at work, and are ultimately less likely to enjoy work, if you do not make time for yourself and/or your loved ones at home to relax and escape from the difficult realities of your work life.

Do whatever is necessary to enjoy your family and/or relax at home. Take vacations. Take days off when you have earned them and/or are entitled to them.

Everyone needs to recharge their batteries from time to time. Make sure that you do whatever is necessary to recharge yours.

Don't Forget to Sleep

An important element for making one's work life more positive, productive and pleasant is to make sure that you get enough sleep each night.

Consider the following example. Rachel is a university professor. She is prolific in her publishing efforts, commonly publishing several lengthy articles per year. In addition, in her ten years as a university professor, she has also published several non-fiction books.

She also routinely teaches several courses per semester and often volunteers to teach in the summer session as well. She is a dedicated teacher/educator and is constantly updating her course materials with cutting-edge developments in her field. She works very long hours year round.

During a typical school year, Rachel commonly gets only four or five hours of sleep per night. Although she is very accomplished in her field, she often feels anxious, nervous, tired, and/or very stressed out.

After getting tenure and teaching at the university level for ten years, she is offered the opportunity to take a six-month sabbatical, which she accepts. She decides to focus her attention during the sabbatical on writing the novel that she always dreamed of writing.

During the sabbatical, Rachel works much more moderate hours. She spends four to six hours per day working on her novel; makes sure that all of her evenings and weekends are free; and, quite by chance, begins to sleep an average of eight hours per night.

Rachel discovers something remarkable during this time. She notices an enormous difference in her energy level; her enthusiasm for her work; her concentration; and her overall efficiency and productivity. She has much more positive energy to put into her work. Her stress level is considerably lower. Her ability to relax and enjoy the non-work aspects of her life is heightened. She has a renewed ability to view all of her daily occurrences in a much more positive light, and has become more playful in how she relates to her family.

* * *

As the Rachel scenario illustrates, most of us *do* in fact function better with the proper amount of sleep. The lesson to be learned from Rachel's example is that additional sleep can make both our home lives and our work lives more positive, productive and pleasant.

* * *

What constitutes the "proper" amount of sleep may vary from person to person, and certainly seems to vary between persons of different ages. As a general matter, however, it seems that many people convince themselves that they *can* function on considerably less sleep than might actually be optimal for them. Simply put, most people gloss over their need for sleep.

The more responsibilities that certain people have in their jobs, the more they convince themselves that the first thing that needs to be sacrificed in order to do their jobs more effectively is their sleep. They believe that they need more waking hours in order to get all of their work done.

Those individuals should be more conscious of the concept of "diminishing returns." Sometimes, you can get more work done in eight hours, coupled with relaxation time and a proper amount of sleep, than you can in twelve hours, without proper rest. Sometimes, working people forget that sufficient sleep day in and day out is critical to minimize overall stress, fatigue, and anxiety. Sometimes, working people forget that sufficient sleep can make them (1) sharper and more productive at work; (2) more likely to be able to successfully manage political issues that may be thrown at them on a daily basis; and (3) more able to make important decisions at work or about work or their careers.

If Rachel's story teaches us anything, it is that having balance in life and getting the proper amount of sleep will in all likelihood make us *more* productive and *more* satisfied and enriched by our work lives. Give a sufficient level of sleep a chance over a period of months and see if it does not make *you* feel more positive, more productive, and less stressed about your overall work situation.

Customer/Client Politics

Another group of individuals who can cause political issues which (1) you may need to deal with at work; and (2) may need to be monitored or managed on a regular basis, are clients and customers of your organization. These are also people with whom you may have indirect working relationships and with whom you need to find a way to get along.

"The Customer Is Always Right"

The fundamental, time-honored principle of customer/client relations which seems to transcend generations of organizational politics is that "the customer is always right." Even today, customer/client relations still seem to begin and end with this approach.

After all, no matter what particular product or service your organization provides, your organization *needs* its customers and clients to continue to purchase those products or services in order for your organization to continue to survive. Customers and clients pay your organization's bills and are its bread and butter. The last thing that you want to do is engage in behavior which has the effect of alienating them.

You must find a way to successfully get along with customers and clients. However, that is sometimes easier said than done. We have all faced situations in which we might disagree with clients' proposed strategies, or where we are certain that our clients are wrong, even though they insist that they are right. We have all faced situations in which customers make unreasonable demands and/or seemingly are never satisfied. The question becomes how to effectively handle the client or customer who presents these challenges.

Consider the following example. Helen is an accountant. One of her long-standing clients is Rita, who owns several antique stores. Over the years, they have had running battles on a variety of financial issues. Helen's advice tends to be fairly conservative and not terribly aggressive. Rita consistently wants to be as aggressive as possible when it comes to tax planning and financial strategies.

In one particular instance, Rita digs in and insists upon taking action that Helen truly believes, based on her years of experience, will backfire in Rita's face. Helen is faced with somewhat of a dilemma. She is certain that Rita's strategy is a mistake. However, if she comes on too strong and tells Rita so, she may alienate Rita and potentially lose her as a client. On the other hand, if she takes a pure "the-client-is-always-right" approach and says nothing, she may not be giving advice which is in her client's best interests and may suffer consequences in any event if Rita's strategy does in fact blow up.

*　　*　　*

How does Helen (and others like her) strike the balance between helping her client and appropriately appeasing her, so that she does not alienate her and ultimately cause her client to seek similar services elsewhere? One short answer to that question is that sometimes you have to relent to the client's wishes, even if you know that you are right, in the overall interest of client relations (unless of course they desire to engage in conduct which you know to be illegal, in which case you may not be able to relent). The client pays you and does not want to constantly argue with you or be told that she is wrong, at least with any degree of regularity. Sometimes, she wants *her* ego stroked. Sometimes, what she wants is for you to find a lawful and creative way to achieve the result that she seeks.

Try to find ways (within legal limits of course) to make the situation or problem work to your client's or customer's advantage. If there are lawful ways to accommodate your client/customer's wishes, try to make every effort to find them. When you have reservations about what a client or customer wants, try to find some common ground between your position and your client's position. In short, try to find creative solutions to the problem.

If you must compromise, or if you simply cannot deliver what your clients or customers desire (or if what they seek to do is illegal), try to explain it in terms that will not alienate or patronize them. Spin it into a positive. Convince them that there is a better way to get what they want and explain why that "better way" is actually in their best interests.

Many times, that type of explanation and/or hand holding may be enough to satisfy even the most demanding clients or customers. Even if they do not ultimately get what they want, if they believe that you are doing everything you can to act in their best interests, that may be enough in some cases to keep them satisfied and/or keep them from leaving you or looking elsewhere for the types of services that you provide.

Discussing Competitors with Clients

Another client relations issue which arises from time to time is one in which you are put in a position in which your client or customer engages you in dialogue about your competitor's prices, products or services. This situation may need to be managed from a client relations perspective as well.

Consider the following example. Iris and Tammy are in

competitive businesses. Both have benefitted from Gerald being a customer of theirs over the years. Both are competing to get a larger volume of business from Gerald. Gerald is also considering giving all of his business to either Iris or Tammy.

Iris and Tammy find themselves in a position in which they are both on the telephone with Gerald, who has asked for input from both of them with respect to a particular problem that he needs to have one of them solve.

Both Tammy and Iris try to impress Gerald. They take different approaches, however. Iris proceeds to badmouth Tammy and Tammy's ideas to Gerald. She thinks that the way to score points with Gerald is to make Iris look as if she does not know what she is doing. Tammy, by contrast, validates the good points that Iris makes; makes no comment at all about the points Iris makes with which she disagrees; tries to keep the conversation with Gerald positive; and makes continuing efforts and suggestions for creative solutions to his problems.

Ultimately, Gerald gives Tammy the project and the lion's share of his business from that point forward. Although he believed that their ideas were equally good, he actually viewed Iris as being more petty and less professional than Tammy and gave Tammy his business for that reason alone.

*   *   *

The Iris/Tammy example illustrates the importance of taking a positive, proactive approach with clients and customers. When you badmouth your competitors to clients and customers, it sometimes can make you look unprofessional and petty. A more positive approach is to extol the virtues of others and give credit where it is due. Doing so can make you look more reasonable, palatable and credible.

Try to put a positive spin on your own skills and talents, rather than denigrate the skills and talents of others. Try to sell from a positive perspective, not from a negative.

"Third Party Contractor" Politics

"Third party contractor" is a generic term that describes any individual or organization that you or your organization pays for products or services that the organization needs to run effectively and efficiently. "Third party contractors" can include (1) law firms that your organization hires to provide legal services; (2) accounting firms that provide your organization with financial or tax advice; (3) public relations firms that provide your organization with publicity opportunities; and/or (4) even individuals or entities who provide copying or fax machines or services for your organization's use, to name just a few.

Sometimes, there are political issues that arise or relationships that need to be effectively managed with "third parties" who work with your organization as well. These "third parties" create the "flip side" to the "the customer is always right" problem. Sometimes, strategies need to be developed to deal with *these* types of individuals and entities when *they* become difficult to work with as well.

Consider the following example. Troy and Evan are brothers. Troy runs a manufacturing business and Evan sells, services, and maintains office copier equipment. Troy has been using Evan's company to service all of his office copying needs (supplying and servicing copy equipment and providing all necessary supplies) for years.

Renee, Troy's office manager, has discovered some problems with using Evan's company to provide copier equipment and service. Upon review of what various competitors provide, Renee discovers that there are other copier companies who offer better prices on service and provide equipment that is more state-of-the-art.

In addition, because Evan's company has grown over the years, he no longer personally handles copier service calls, but has a staff of people whom he has hired to handle them for him. Renee has been very unsatisfied with the quality of the service that her company receives from Evan's company; the timeliness of the service responses; and the attitude of some of the individuals who actually come out to make the service calls.

Renee is faced with somewhat of a dilemma. She needs to communicate to Troy that she is unsatisfied with Evan's level of service, but cannot outright seek new copier service elsewhere because Evan is Troy's brother. She knows that Troy will never allow her to terminate his contract with Evan. Nor will he be receptive to hearing criticisms about his brother or his brother's company.

Renee needs to find a way to manage this problem. She needs to appease her boss; get along with Evan; and find a non-offensive way to communicate to Evan that (1) his service people are not terribly responsive and (2) there are competitors who are offering better service than his company is.

One factor that she has going for her is that Evan's company needs to make sure that *it* gets along with *its* clients and that *its* clients are satisfied. Even if Renee cannot threaten Evan with changing copier service companies, she might still be able to communicate that the service that he is providing is substandard and that he might lose *other* accounts if he is not careful. If Evan is a savvy businessperson, he might take Renee's input seriously; the services she receives might actually improve; and Renee might not have to alienate either Evan or Troy at all.

$$* \quad * \quad *$$

The Evan/Troy/Renee scenario reinforces two critical points to understand when attempting to get along with "third party contractors." First, "third parties" provide your organization with a service that it *need*s. For that reason, you cannot afford to completely alienate them. Rather, you *do* need to make your best efforts to try to successfully work with them.

Some key strategies for effectively dealing with these individuals and organizations are as follows. Communicate directly with them. Make sure that they understand exactly what it is that you need. Compliment them. Make sure that they know when you are satisfied with them. Compromise when necessary. Always work with an eye toward working out the details of your working relationship with them, rather than antagonizing them.

Second, understand that "third party contractors" also need *you* and ultimately *work* for *you*. Remember that their philosophy and attitude toward *you* also needs to be that "the customer is always right." *You* are their customer. They need to make efforts to get along with *you* and members of your organization as well. They need to understand that if they are too contrary or disagreeable with *you*, they run the risk of losing *you* as a customer.

*   *   *

In short, if you deal with "third party contractors" on a regular basis at work, try to do your best to get along with them and to keep them motivated to *want* to assist you and your organization. The better that you can get along with these "third parties," and the more motivated that they are, the more positive your overall work experience can be.

PART FOUR

Contending with Various Personalities at Work

CHAPTER 10

The Bully

This Chapter addresses workplace "bullies," those unpleasant people who seem to go out of their way to make your work experience miserable and/or elevate themselves at your expense. We have all been subjected to bullies at work at one time or another.

The good news is that there *are* ways to minimize the potentially negative effects of workplace bullies and turn the negative experience of dealing with them into a positive. What follows are (1) some tips regarding how to recognize and perhaps even *understand* workplace bullies to some degree; and (2) some suggestions for effectively handling them at your workplace.

Who Is the Workplace Bully?

There are a several types of bullies that you might encounter at the workplace. The bullies that you face may possess one or a combination of the following "bullying" traits.

First, there is the "schoolyard" variety of bully. These bullies are individuals who prey on people whom they perceive to be weaker than they are (or have less power than they do). The "schoolyard" bullies prey on others to make themselves appear stronger. Although these bullies try to create the appearance of being supremely confident, they rarely are. Rather, they are commonly quite insecure.

In an actual "schoolyard," the conventional wisdom for responding to these individuals is either to ignore them if possible or to be right back in their face. In the *workplace*, however, these strategies are not likely to be very effective against this type of bully. The reason is that the "schoolyard" type of bully who commonly works with you tends to be either *your* supervisor or *a* supervisor; tends *not* to back down; tends *not* to be easily intimidated; and/or usually is someone with whom you *must* interact on a regular basis.

A second type of bully is the "angry" bully. Angry bullies tend to enjoy arguing with people and seem to *look* for reasons to pick fights. They can be quite negative and even bitter at times; as well as insulting and patronizing. They are commonly aware that they are not very popular at their workplaces, which can make them even more angry and bitter. They may have some power, although frequently not as much as they would like others to believe they have, which might contribute to their anger as well.

Finally, there are the "defensive" bullies. These individuals hate to be told that they are wrong about anything and hate even more to be *proven* wrong. They also can often be quite insecure, particularly about their workplace knowledge, skills, and abilities in certain areas.

It is unlikely that you will hear "defensive" bullies *admit* that they are wrong or that they made a mistake. They are far more likely to make excuses, tell wild tales, or blame others when directly confronted with their mistakes or shortcomings. They also have been known to flat out lie when they feel cornered or particularly vulnerable.

The more wrong defensive bullies are or *know* they are, the more defensive and bullying they are likely to be. The bullying behavior is a mechanism for "saving face," which they commonly believe they need to do.

Suggested Strategies for Dealing with Workplace Bullies

There are several affirmative steps that you can take (and behaviors you might want to avoid) to effectively contend with any and all types of bullies at your workplace. Some of these strategies are designed to be responsive to the immediacy of a bullying attack, while others are designed to be implemented as longer term strategies.

Short-Term Strategies

Avoid Engaging the Bully in Argument

One suggestion for handling workplace bullies in the immediate moment of the bullying is not to participate in the argument to the extent possible or beyond what is absolutely necessary to extricate yourself from the immediacy of the situation. You are not likely to win the argument or make any meaningful points with these individuals at those moments anyway. Simply let them vent and concede the legitimate points that they are making at the time.

As was noted in Chapter 5, most people have an instinct to argue when being argued with and/or to fight back defensively when provoked. However, responding in kind to a bully, particularly at the moment that you are being bullied, is not likely to get you what you ultimately want, and *is* likely to make you frustrated and angry.

Being confrontational at that level, even if you *are* successful at causing the person to back down at that moment, is extremely stressful and uncomfortable. That level of contentiousness is certainly not likely to make your work environment more positive or pleasant.

In addition, remember that bullies are often more skilled at bullying than you are. If you take on bullies on their terms, you will likely end up fueling the fire; feeling bullied further; and/or feeling worse than if you had not taken them on at all.

Further, if the bullies happen to be your supervisors, bullying them back is likely to inflame them further and perhaps even alienate them. Although supervisors certainly do not have the *right* to mistreat, yell at, or abuse anyone at their workplace, you need to remember that they *do* have the power to make your life at work miserable; as well as the ability to evaluate your performance and recommend you for raises or promotions. The last thing you want at work, whatever your goals, is to alienate a person who has that kind of potential control or power over your fate, particularly if that individual is a bully and might be likely to hold a grudge against you.

Try to avoid the temptation during a bullying attack of telling the workplace bully/supervisor off. Although great come-back lines are the stuff that good movies are made of, in the real-life workplace, you are far less likely to get what you want out of your job or your supervisor if you use them. The short-term satisfaction from telling the bully/supervisor to go jump in a lake (or using considerably stronger language to that effect), is very likely to make matters worse for you and have long-lasting negative effects on your overall working environment.

Tell Them How They Make You Feel

Another suggestion for dealing specifically with bullying attacks themselves relates to instances of bullying which leave you feeling offended, abused, or as if you have been treated unfairly. You *will* likely need to do something about those feelings at some point. These types of issues usually need to be talked out and resolved.

With a bully, however, timing is everything. You will need to *patiently* wait for an opportunity to present your concerns to the bullies directly (or to others if you need to make a more formal complaint about their behavior) at a moment when they are calmer and perhaps less defensive and more reasonable.

Be prepared for that discussion. You want to appear calm, intelligent and reasonable yourself when presenting your version of the event. If necessary, shortly after the unpleasant event occurs, jot down some notes for yourself, so that your recollection of the event can be refreshed and that you can present a detailed account, with examples, of your version of what happened and why it is troubling to you.

Long-Term Strategies

Get to Know the Bully on a Personal Level

One suggestion for minimizing the number of bullying instances that you may be subjected to long-term at your workplace is to develop more of a personal relationship with the bully, if you possibly can and/or if you possibly can stand it. Remember, bullies are people too. They have feelings, interests, and goals, just like you. (Well, maybe not just like you, but they do have feelings, interests and goals.)

Over time, try to engage bullies in conversation about their personal likes and dislikes. You might find that you have common interests. If you make efforts to discuss those shared interests with the bullies, your exchanges with them might be more pleasant and perhaps your overall work experience might be more enjoyable. You might even find that the bully is actually a likeable person when relaxed and not feeling defensive or backed into a corner.

The work-related effect of establishing this type of personal connection can be very positive as well. Remember, one of the ultimate goals here is to be able to effectively and productively work with bullies and to address and resolve work-related problems with them when they arise. Developing a personal relationship with a bullying individual can (1) motivate the individual to *want* to help you when a work-related problem arises;

(2) make the bullying episodes less frequent and easier to deal with when they do occur; (3) enable you to talk through problem areas with the bully more productively and effectively; and (4) disarm the bully, which, in turn, is likely to make him or her less defensive overall.

Talk to Them When They Are Likely to Be Relaxed

Still another strategy for effectively dealing with bullies long term is to figure out their pattern (if there is one) of highs and lows during the course of an average workday and try to talk to them during times when they are in a better mood. If, for example, they are morning people, try to have discussions with them in the mornings. On the other hand, if they tend to be busier, more distracted, anxious or stressed out in the mornings because they are handling more workplace issues during those times, be aware that they may also be more likely to engage in bullying behaviors during those times. In that situation, try to have work-related discussions with them later in the day.

In any event, try to discuss important issues with these types of individuals when they tend to be calmer; more reasonable; more likely to be receptive to talking; and perhaps even more motivated to work through your issues. You may discover that you are much more able to reason with them at those times than you thought that you would be. In fact, you may even discover that they are considerably less negative during those times, which could maximize the effectiveness and productivity of your discussions.

(Note, however, that issues may arise from time to time which *do* require more prompt attention or a more prompt response. In those instances, you may need to address or confront bullies during times when they might not be at their best. If that occurs, you will have to force yourself to address those issues at those inopportune times. In those instances, try to (1) be very well-prepared for those discussions; (2) anticipate problem areas and questions and be ready to discuss them intelligently, reasonably, and in depth if necessary; (3) avoid "chit chatty" dialogue with them at those particular times; and (4) narrow the issues to only those that require immediate attention at those times. In a continuing effort to display patience, try to save non-urgent issues for discussions at other times, perhaps later in the day or week.)

*   *   *

In short, it *is* possible to have a positive work experience, and get what you want from your job, even if you *do* have to contend with one or more bullies from time to time. The keys are to recognize the bullies; understand what motivates them to act the way that they do; and respond accordingly.

CHAPTER 11

The Screamer

This Chapter addresses workplace "screamers," those seemingly out of control individuals who raise their voices on a regular basis at work. As we all know, the screaming sessions are often unprovoked and unpredictable, and are almost always unpleasant.

What follows are (1) some tips regarding how to recognize and perhaps even *understand* workplace screamers to some degree; and (2) some suggestions for effectively handling them at your workplace.

Who Is the Workplace Screamer?

Screamers are cousins to bullies, who were addressed in Chapter 10. Screamers are often high-strung, not particularly calm, individuals. They respond to workplace stresses, mistakes and unanticipated problems by yelling. The yelling is commonly driven by sheer frustration and often times appears in the form of an uncontrolled outburst.

There are some obvious similarities between screamers and bullies, most notably that both tend to be aggressive in their tone and behavior. One distinction between them, however, is that screamers do not necessarily need to "flex" at the moment of the screaming. Unlike bullies, who, as noted in Chapter 10, can selectively prey on individuals whom they perceive to be in a position of weakness relative to them (and who will rarely attempt to bully their superiors at the workplace), screamers seem to be far less calculating and far more emotional. In addition, screamers are commonly of the "equal opportunity" variety, *i.e.*, people who scream at everyone, subordinates, colleagues and superiors alike.

The good news is that screamers commonly have no real personal axe to grind with the individuals whom they scream at. Sometimes, they say things during outbursts that they may not even remember saying later when in calmer moments.

Finally, screamers usually do not mean to personally insult anyone. More often than not, people who get screamed at just happen to be in the way of screamers at their moments of frustration.

Suggested Strategies for Dealing with Workplace Screamers

Most people at your workplace, including at times the screamers themselves, would probably agree that screaming behavior is unacceptable and that no one should be subjected to such behavior at the workplace. Getting "screamed" at at work can not only be humiliating, but can also be very demoralizing and unmotivating.

If these are your feelings in response to being screamed at, you are not alone. You (and others who suffer from these indignities) will likely need to talk to the screamers at some point to let them know how their screaming makes you feel. The following strategies involve how and when to have these conversations.

(In addition, please note that several of the strategies for effectively dealing with bullies at the workplace might also have useful application for working with screamers. In that regard, please refer to the detailed discussions of those strategies in Chapter 10.)

Pick the Right Time of Day and the Right Mood

As with bullies, one effective strategy for responding to screamers might be to pick the right time of day, when they are in the right mood in which to have discussions about their antics. In short, make sure that you approach screamers when they are calmer and more reasonable.

Be Direct

Be aware that screamers may ultimately be *easier* to talk with about these issues in their calmer moments than bullies. Unlike in the case of bullies, who may be uncomfortable admitting that they were wrong or that they even *have* a weakness, you may be able to be more *direct* with screamers in your confrontations about their behavior.

Screamers typically *know* that screaming is one of their weaknesses. Because they might even be a little embarrassed by their behavior, you may ultimately be able to have a productive conversation, and even get an apology, when discussing these issues with them directly, as long as you pick the right moment for the discussion and avoid making them defensive about their behavior.

Making It Personal

One way to avoid making screamers defensive when trying to talk out an issue of this sort is to make the issue personal from your perspective. For example, try telling them how the screaming and insulting makes you feel, citing perhaps to specific language that the screamer used during the outburst. Because, in many cases, the screamers did not *mean* the remarks to be personal, and actually may even respect you more than you realize, identifying the reasons that you took the discussion personally might actually disarm the screamers to some degree. It may turn out that they feel badly on a personal level that you interpreted their remarks the way that you did.

Take caution in using this approach, however. Certainly, you need to make a judgment call in each instance as to whether this kind of "personal" approach will work with your particular screamer. Generally, if you have observed that your screamers have an unselfish "human" side, or if they have a reputation for ultimately being fair, they might respond well to this type of approach.

Being "In-Their-Face"

The "personal" approach may be *less* likely to work in response to a screamer whom you perceive to be less fair, less sensitive, and perhaps more egocentric. For these types of screamers, a "being right back in their face" strategy might be an appropriate one. What this usually means is to be direct, and stand your ground firmly and clearly, *during the actual moment of the screaming.* (It does not necessarily mean that you should scream back at them. It is usually not helpful or productive to scream back at anyone at the workplace. Doing so commonly does nothing but inflame the situation further. For more discussion of how to handle inflamed situations at work, please also see Chapter 5.)

Take caution with this approach as well, however. If these individuals are supervisors, or your supervisors in particular, you obviously will need to pick those fights *very* carefully and not too often.

The reason that a more "in your face" strategy might work with the more aggressive, less personal, less sensitive screamers, is that they are commonly accustomed to relating to people in a screaming manner. They sometimes actually respond *better* to people who are aggressive and animated with them than to people who are polite and soft spoken.

They might even have more respect for the aggressiveness since *they* tend to be aggressive and impolite themselves. It is quite possible that these types of individuals tend to see politeness and gentle approaches as signs of weakness.

Avoid Discussions with Screamers in Front of Co-Workers

Whatever conversation you ultimately choose to have with your workplace screamers, but particularly those confronting the "in-their-face" types, try to talk in private if possible, rather than in hallways or common areas. Animated, loud conversations tend to draw attention. Co-workers commonly only hear bits and pieces of these conversations and often can make incorrect or incomplete judgments based on what they *think* they hear, to say nothing of the fact that such types of conversations can be embarrassing at times.

Even if your conversations with screamers prove to be productive, your co-workers may not perceive it that way. The last thing that you want is for unsubstantiated, negative rumors about you to be floating around your workplace, particularly when they are incorrectly based upon conversations that were otherwise positive.

* * *

In short, there are a number of options for successfully resolving conflicts with workplace screamers. Understanding that the screamers' remarks toward you are typically not personal may go a long way toward making your working relationship with screamers a bit more pleasant (or at least easier to deal with).

CHAPTER 12

The Charming Backstabber

This Chapter addresses "charming backstabbers," those seemingly delightful people who can support and praise you to your face, but "badmouth" or hurt you for their own personal or political benefit behind your back. Unfortunately, everyone has been exposed to the backstabbers at some point during their work life. As we all know, these individuals can be dangerous if you do not have strategies in place for working effectively with them.

The goal of this Chapter is to minimize the negative effects that the charming backstabbers might have on you at work. What follows are (1) some tips regarding how to recognize charming backstabbers; and (2) some suggestions not only for effectively working with them directly, but also for neutralizing their effects on your overall work situation.

Who Is the Charming Backstabber?

The basic profile of charming backstabbers is that they are typically friendly and charming on the outside, the kinds of people who commonly tell stories; are funny; and/or are seemingly fun to be with. They are popular at work. Before we know better, many of us *want* to gravitate to, talk to, befriend, and even open up to, these types of individuals.

Be cautious about them, however. Just because someone's office, desk, or work station might be near yours and that individual can be disarming and/or fun to be with, does not mean that he or she is trustworthy.

Charming backstabbers might flatter you to your face by being supportive; enthusiastic about issues you discuss; encouraging; and perhaps even complimentary of your work at times. However, they are also people who sometimes do *not* keep your confidences; *may* use your confidences and any other information they obtain about you to gain advantage for themselves if they can or if they perceive it to be necessary; can be quite self-centered; and ultimately seem to be largely loyal only to themselves.

In addition, understand that charming backstabbers can be manipulative and persistent. They can seduce us with their charms and then use those charms to get what they want. They often find charming ways to convince us to say "yes," even when we *want* to say "no."

Most of us do not want to *believe* that these individuals *are* backstabbers or that they are capable of backstabbing *us*. However, backstabbers sometimes depend on our trusting instincts to help them to get what they want, for as long as we will let them.

Sometimes, the only way to discover that someone *is* a backstabber is to have the unfortunate firsthand experience of being "stabbed" yourself or, at a minimum, to observe someone else being "attacked" by that individual. Even then, the first time that you are "stabbed in the back," you are often not sure what happened. Since you were not actually *present* for the behind-your-back stabbing, and either heard about it secondhand or felt some vague effects from it, it is common to second-guess what you think *may* have happened. For this reason, it may take one, two or even a few instances of actual backstabbing to conclude that the charming individual is in fact also a backstabber.

Suggested Strategies for Dealing with Charming Backstabbers

Once you discover that individuals *are* backstabbers, no matter how charming they may be outwardly, your guard should go up. However, that is not to say that you cannot work effectively with these people, both in the short run and, if necessary, over the long-term. What follows are some suggested strategies for (1) protecting yourself *before* you are sure that someone *is* a backstabber; (2) dealing with the backstabbing situation once you *know* that it is likely to occur; and (3) working effectively and successfully with backstabber personality types.

Protecting Yourself

Learn Whom to Trust

A preliminary strategy for responding to co-workers and supervisors alike at work is to be cautious about whom you trust, at least initially. Be wary, for example, of people who are *too* effusive with you or about you, particularly if they do not know you very well. The effusiveness may not be real and these individuals may turn out to be backstabbers.

In addition, be patient about the relationships that you develop at work. Get to know the people that you work with slowly. If you do, presumably you will develop better instincts about whom to trust and will be less likely to befriend or trust individuals who turn out to be charming backstabbers.

Learn When to Share Your Confidences

Try to get to know people *before* providing them with personal or private information about yourself, or with your confidences or other information which could hurt you if disseminated to the wrong people in your organization. Sometimes, that is easier said than done. Many of us want to make friends at work. Sometimes, we cannot help ourselves when it comes to sharing intimate details about our personal lives or confidences relating to work with others whom we perceive to be close to us. For your own protection, try to resist the temptation to do so.

However, if you *are* a person who instinctively *does* reveal confidences to people sooner than perhaps you should, at least try to be judicious about the information you dole out by giving it out a little at a time. For example, if you *must* provide people with some private information about yourself before you get to know them well, try to limit the information you give them to what you would not mind everyone in your organization knowing. If that information gets disseminated around your organization, the individuals who spread it will have shown their true colors. Presumably, from that point forward, you will recognize that these are not individuals whom you should befriend or whom you can trust with other, perhaps more sensitive, information or issues.

On the other hand, if the little bit of information you initially provide remains confidential, you may develop an increased comfort level with the individuals to whom you gave that information. At that point, you can provide those individuals with a little more information if you so choose. Then, see how well those individuals do in keeping that information confidential.

By doling out information a little at a time and learning whom you can trust slowly, you will increase your chances of not trusting too soon or getting "burned" by someone who turns out to be a charming backstabber.

Dealing with Charming Backstabbers Directly

What follows are several suggestions for effectively dealing directly with charming backstabbers, and certain behaviors to avoid, in your effort to minimize backstabbing which might be directed toward you. Remember, you have to find ways to *work* with these people, in order to make your own work experience positive and productive.

Convince the Backstabbers
that You Are on Their Side

Try to impress the charming backstabbers with your work and attitude. Try to do all of the work that they ask of you, without complaint or any indication that you do not want to or cannot. Make them believe that you are "in their camp" and that you are a team player. Backstabbers are less likely to stab you in the back if they are happy with your work; think that you are on their team; think that your goal is to succeed for them and make them look good; believe that you are *not* a threat; and believe that you are giving them what they want.

Avoid Letting on that You Know
They Are Backstabbers

Try to avoid letting the backstabbers become aware that you *know* who they really are or that you *know* what they do or are capable of doing. Many of us have an instinct, for example, to *inform* backstabbers that we "understand them better than they think we do" or that we are "on to them."

Try to resist the temptation to make this kind of remark to a backstabber because, even though it might make you feel better in the short run, it often can be a mistake. The charming backstabbers' perception of their powers resides in part in their manipulative ability to charm people into doing what they want, without others realizing that they are being manipulated.

The last thing that charming backstabbers want to learn is that someone is "on to" their tactics. They may redouble their efforts to stab those individuals in the back, to eliminate what they perceive to be a threat to themselves or their stature within the organization. They may find new ways that you could not have possibly anticipated to hurt you, which will, of course, make your work experience even more difficult. (On the other hand, as was noted earlier in the Chapter, be aware that backstabbers are less likely to engage in these behaviors if they do *not* view you as a threat or if they *do* perceive you to be a loyal employee who either is "in their camp" or is someone whom they were successful at charming or manipulating.)

Avoid Confrontations about Specific Incidents

In addition, try not to confront charming backstabbers directly about any specific, alleged backstabbing incident. Their response may likely be unpleasant.

First, they are certainly likely to deny that they stabbed you or anyone else in the back. They may remain charming, supportive and complimentary, at least to your face. They might do everything that they can to convince you that they are telling you the truth; that you are wrong; that you did not observe what you *think* you did; and that you can, in fact, trust them. Their denial may cause you to question your judgment or make you less confident or trusting of your own instincts, which is what they want.

Second, when confronted with a direct accusation that they stabbed you or someone else, backstabbers may likely *now* view you as a threat, even if they did not before. Whatever image they present to your face, they may be likely, once again, to become even more defensive behind your back and step up their efforts to hurt you. Those efforts could involve convincing others that you are a problem or a trouble-making employee, whether that is based in truth or not.

Remember, these individuals are *backstabbers*. They are capable of lying to you and others to get what they want.

Never Trust Backstabbers

Once you know that the people you are working with are in fact backstabbers, *never* trust or rely on them to support you, fight for you, or assist you in achieving your goals. They often may not support you unless they perceive that it is in their own best interests to do so.

Be Careful When Complaining About Backstabbers

Be careful when you complain to others about charming backstabbers. Make sure that, if you *do* complain, you complain to people whom you *can* completely trust.

Suppose, for example, that the backstabber has a close relationship with the person to whom you complain. Be aware that there are several possible negative consequences which could result from your complaint. The complaint might not be taken seriously. The backstabber may be informed of your complaint in terms which are not particularly flattering to you and may increase his or her efforts to hurt you further. The person you complain to may also be a backstabber, which unwittingly puts you in a position in which you have to watch out for the negative actions of two people, rather than one.

In short, if you *do* complain, make sure that (1) you do not put yourself in a position in which you are *worse* off than if you had not complained; and (2) the complaint is likely to *help* you in getting the issue resolved.

Neutralizing the Effects of Charming Backstabbers

Although you may need to do *some* work with backstabbers, one way to neutralize the impact of the backstabbing on your overall work situation is to work with and gain the support of others at your workplace, if that is at all possible. There are two strategies for accomplishing this.

Avoid Working Exclusively for Backstabbers

Try not to allow yourself to be in a position in which you work *exclusively* for backstabbers, even for a short period of time. If you find yourself working exclusively, or even predominantly, for a backstabber, try to extricate yourself from that situation if you can. Seek a transfer to another department if that is available to you or try to cultivate working relationships with other "power players" in the organization.

The reason is that, even if you manage to convince backstabbers that you are an ally over the short term, at the first sign that you have done *anything* which is in any way inconsistent with the backstabbers' agendas or goals (which is inevitable), you may be stabbed in the back anyway. If you are not working with anyone else, there will be no one to protect you once the backstabbing begins.

Reduce Your Workload for Them Over Time

Little by little, try to reduce (and ultimately even eliminate if possible) the amount of work that you do with backstabbers by working more and more for others in your organization over time. The more people you work with in your organization and the more allies you develop at your workplace, the less impactful backstabbers' negative comments about you will be and the less likely that any one backstabber will be able to cause extensive damage to you.

A long-term goal here is to create a situation in which people within your organization who have the independent ability to make decisions which could impact on your work life are so pleased with you and your work that they are not likely to be influenced by negative or backstabbing remarks made about you.

One way to succeed at getting others in your organization, particularly those whom you admire, respect and trust and/or who are in a position of power or influence, to give you work and support you is to offer at every opportunity to help them. Seek them out. Try to impress them by "doing the work" and having a positive attitude. Do everything possible to continue to cultivate those relationships over time.

If backstabbers' work interferes with other work that you view as more important for your long-term stability in your organization, inform your *supporters* of the conflict. Let them know that you would be *happy* to do their work if you could somehow be relieved of your responsibilities for the backstabbers. Encourage them to make arrangements with the backstabbers directly to relieve you of those other responsibilities.

Of course, in order for your supporters to go to bat for you in this way, you will need them to *continue* to support you over the long run and continue to believe that you are invaluable to them. That involves not only doing the work successfully and maintaining a positive attitude over time, but also making sure that you do your necessary politicking with them on an ongoing basis. Make sure that everyone continues to know, for example, what you are working on and what a good job you are doing.

As always, you will need to be patient with respect to this strategy. Developing meaningful, long-lasting bonds with people at the workplace who can support and assist you takes time.

What If My Supervisor Is a Charming Backstabber?

In circumstances in which you *cannot* seek a transfer or manage to extricate yourself from a situation over the long-term in which you work with a backstabber, a critical question becomes "How do I best work with a backstabber who happens to be my supervisor?" The key in that situation is to figure out ways to get along and work effectively with that individual.

Be assured that, even if your supervisor is a backstabber, you can be successful and productive in working with him or her. Try to make use of most of the strategies which have been discussed throughout this Chapter.

For example, be pleasant. Be guarded. Protect yourself. Try to avoid completely trusting that individual. Do your best to convince your boss that you are not a threat, but rather are loyal to him or her. "Do the work." Do what he or she asks of you with minimal or no complaining. Try to stay on his or her good side. Make your boss believe that you are in his or her camp. Be supportive. Listen when he or she complains about others, but try not to take sides if possible.

*   *   *

In short, try not to give charming backstabbers a *reason* to stab you in the back. Remember, in most workplaces, people do not stab each other in the back merely for "sport." More often than not, backstabbers will not go out of their way to hurt other individuals unless they perceive there to be a threat to their own security or that they will somehow gain a great advantage by doing so. If you take away backstabbers' *reasons* for wanting or needing to hurt you, they might be less likely to do so, which of course will make working for or with them easier, more pleasant, less threatening, and potentially more positive.

CHAPTER 13

Catherine the Ruthless

This Chapter addresses "ruthless" individuals at the workplace, those abrasive persons who tend to "step on" people who get in the way of what they want. The ruthless individual (who shall be referred to in this Chapter as "Catherine") is one of the more dangerous personality types you may encounter at work.

The goal of this Chapter is to minimize the negative effects that Catherine the Ruthless can have on your overall work situation. What follows are (1) some tips for how to recognize her; and (2) some suggestions for working effectively with her.

Who Is Catherine the Ruthless?

This personality type is often not very hard to spot at the workplace. Catherine is very clear and direct about what she wants and makes it equally clear that she has little use for anyone who cannot continually assist her in getting what she wants.

What *does* Catherine the Ruthless want? Typically, her primary concerns are money and power. She can be relentless in her pursuit of those things.

Catherine is the most openly and unapologetically self-centered of all of the personality types. Her motto is "What is in it for me?" She is often quite confident with a large ego, which needs to be stroked on a regular basis. She gets petulant when people say "no" to her or when she does not get what she wants. Sometimes, she may even go out of her way to make sure that individuals who do not help her to achieve her goals "pay the proverbial price," particularly over the long run.

Unlike the charming backstabber, who commonly "glad hands" you to your face and then stabs you in the back, the ruthless personality is capable of stabbing you while you watch. There is often little that Catherine will not do, within legal parameters, to obtain wealth and/or maintain her power base. She is willing to cut you or others off at the knees, seemingly without second thoughts or remorse, if she perceives that you or they are in the way of her getting what she wants.

Nor will Catherine commonly allow personalities, personal relationships, or emotion to get in her way. It often does not matter whether she has a personal affinity for you or not. It appears that she does not care whether she is liked or disliked by co-workers or subordinates, as long as they continue to assist her in achieving her goals. She even seems capable at times of turning on her closest colleagues, if she believes that it is necessary to do so.

Sometimes, Catherine also can be vicious and mean-spirited. She tends to regard politeness and gentle approaches as signs of weakness; and sometimes pokes fun at individuals whom she perceives to be weak, or at least weaker than she is.

Finally, Catherine tends to be aggressive and is often openly proud of it. If you apologize to her for any reason, she may very well go for the jugular. In her world, it is (figuratively) "kill or be killed." In addition, she seems convinced these traits and her corresponding behaviors are the *only* behaviors which can or will help her get ahead. She sometimes does not even seem to realize that there *are* acceptable alternative behaviors at the workplace.

Suggested Strategies for Effectively Dealing with Catherine the Ruthless

There are a number of suggested strategies for dealing with Catherine the Ruthless at work. Several of these strategies are similar to those discussed at length in Chapter 12 as strategies for successfully responding to charming backstabbers.

"Do the Work"

One important strategy for dealing with ruthless personalities at work is to do the work; work hard; and do the work well. Catherine appreciates people who work extremely hard; make money for her; and have many successes. The more successes that you have and the more money that you make for her, the less likely that she will feel the need to ruthlessly bring you down.

There is a point of caution here, however. You should note that it is common for Catherine not to be completely satisfied. She always wants more *for* herself and *from* others. She certainly is capable of second-guessing your judgment calls; can be quite critical of and unforgiving about any mistakes that others make; and sometimes will blame others even for her *own* mistakes, particularly if she feels threatened.

In light of these tendencies, one way to avoid the wrath of Catherine the Ruthless is to do the work well and to be very conscious at all times of keeping your mistakes, particularly on critically important projects, to a minimum.

Avoid Turning Her Down

The last thing that you want to do if you can avoid it is to get on Catherine's bad side. Remember, she is ruthless and unforgiving.

One way to get on her bad side is to create an impression in Catherine that you crossed her or attempted to cross her. She usually will not stand for this, which might motivate her to exact a "price" from you. For this reason, unless you have strong support in your organization and are confident of the outcome, try to avoid crossing or even underestimating Catherine.

Another way to get on Catherine's bad side is to say "no" to her for any work-related reason or turn down assignments when she gives them to you. No matter how well you have performed for Catherine in the past, she tends to show little loyalty if you do not continue to perform well for her and continue to assist her in getting what she wants.

The question that she is likely to ask herself about you is "What have you done for me lately?" If Catherine believes that you have done *nothing* to help her achieve her goals or make her look good *very recently*, she is capable of disposing of you (figuratively) or making your life miserable (literally).

If it is absolutely necessary that you turn down Catherine when she tries to give you work, inform her about the work you are doing which precludes you from doing hers. Try to encourage her and the others for whom you are doing work to resolve the conflicts amongst themselves and then to give you clear direction regarding whose work is to take priority.

Be prepared, however, for Catherine to respond to you by indicating that you are required to do her work despite the conflict and despite the herculean effort you will have to put forth in order to get *all* of the work, hers and others', done well. If Catherine takes that position, you may have no choice, at least in the short run, but to do all of her work. The success strategy in that instance might be a longer term one of working with and gaining the support of others in the organization over time, if you can. (More about how to extricate yourself from working with Catherine appears later in the Chapter.)

Convince Catherine that You Are "Just Like Her"

People tend to gravitate to and be most comfortable with individuals whom they perceive to have common goals as and similar personalities to themselves. It validates their behavior and makes them want to spend time with those individuals and perhaps even support or help them.

This concept has no better application than in the context of Catherine the Ruthless. Try to ingratiate yourself to Catherine by convincing her that you are just like her (to the extent possible). Try, for example, to convince her that you possess the same traits that she does; that you have the same priorities that she has; that you view the world in the same way that she does; that you are as ambitious as she is; that you desire to treat people in the same manner that she does; and that you understand that doing so is the best way to get what you want.

Catherine *wants* to befriend individuals who are aggressive and ruthless. Because she believes that her behaviors are appropriate and justified, she *needs* to be validated by, and *wants* to surround herself with, people who share her point of view. She *wants* to hear war stories from individuals who "stuck" it to others. She responds *best* to individuals whom she perceives to be as aggressive as she is.

Neutralize Catherine by Working with Others

As was the case with the charming backstabbers, another way to minimize the negative effects of ruthless people at your workplace is to work with a variety of people, if you can. Once again, the more people you work with in your organization, and, in particular, the more friends in high places you make whom you can trust to support and protect you, the less impactful Catherine is likely to be on your overall work life.

The key here, as it was with the charming backstabbers, is to work hard; impress others; and ingratiate yourself to others at your workplace. The goal is to minimize the damage that Catherine can wield toward you and minimize the blame that she can place on you for mistakes.

In addition, if you *do* have to do work with Catherine, it is a good idea to inform others of what specific projects you are working on with Catherine and the extent of your involvement on those projects. If any of the work with Catherine, or your relationship with Catherine, goes south, at least you will have done what you could to set yourself up to minimize the blame that you will have to take from her, at least in the eyes of your other supporters in your organization. (Please refer again to Chapter 12 for more of a detailed discussion of how to neutralize the negative impact of a strong personality type such as this.)

Stay Out of Catherine's Way

Because Catherine can be ruthless in her demands and in her wrath, you will want to stay out of her way as much as possible. Not only does this mean minimizing the amount of work that you do with her and insulating yourself from her, but it also means getting out of her way when she is attacking someone else.

Catherine the Ruthless can be like a runaway train. If you get in her way (or impede her path toward getting what she wants), look out. She might bring you down along with all others in her path. Stay out of her way unless you absolutely have to take her on and, even then, proceed with caution and with the support of other influential people at work in doing so, if you possibly can.

Never Trust Her

Finally, try not to ever put yourself in a position in which you need to depend on, rely on, or trust Catherine for support or to fight on your behalf. She commonly is not likely to do so.

Remember that Catherine will *always* act in a manner which she perceives to be in her *own* best interests and which she perceives will maximize her chances of getting what *she* wants. Even if you are in her good graces at a given moment in time, her actions are usually not *intended* to benefit anyone but her. Sometimes, her actions may *happen* to benefit you. Other times they may not. You certainly cannot and should not *rely* on her to act with any level of consistency to protect or support *your* best interests.

Further, even if you *do* happen to be in Catherine's good graces at a particular moment in time, there is no assurance that her positive impression of you will last for any length of time. Like the charming backstabber, Catherine the Ruthless is capable of turning on you without hesitation or remorse if she believes that it is in her best interests to do so or that it is not in her best interests to protect you.

* * *

In short, Catherine the Ruthless is not the profile of an individual whom you can or should trust with respect to any work-related issue that is important to you. However, you can make your work situation a positive one even if you do have to work with Catherine. The best ways to deal with her are to impress her; stay on her good side; and minimize the degree to which you need to rely on her to help you get what *you* want.

CHAPTER 14

Control Freaks and Nitpickers

This Chapter addresses workplace "control freaks" and "nitpickers." Control freaks are those individuals who micromanage every detail of their jobs, your job, and everyone else's job. Nitpickers are a subset of control freaks and exercise a particular form of control. They are those individuals who cannot resist pointing out every mistake that you make, every time that you make one. Usually, the control freaks and nitpickers who tend to have the most impact on your work life are those who either supervise you directly or supervise others with whom you work.

The goal of this Chapter is to minimize the negative effects that control freaks and nitpickers might have on you at work. What follows are (1) some tips regarding how to recognize control freaks and nitpickers; and (2) some suggestions for effectively and productively working with them.

Who Are the Control Freaks?

We have all worked with control freaks. Typically, their view of the work world is that they can do the job at hand better, more effectively, and more efficiently than those who work for or with them.

They have a compelling need to make sure that the job is "done right," according to their unique vision of what "done right" means. They will either oversee every detail of a project to ensure that it *is* done right, or will simply take over the project and do it themselves. In any event, they like to place their proverbial "stamp" on every item of work product which goes out under their supervision.

Control freaks often do not know *how* to delegate tasks to others; are *afraid* to delegate; or simply *refuse* to delegate. When they *do* delegate, they tend to do so only when their backs are to the wall and/or they are totally overloaded themselves. When they *do* delegate, they still try to keep as much control over projects as they possibly can.

In addition, when they delegate, control freaks tend not to be very effective communicators, which can compound the control problem. Without proper direction or effective communication with respect to precisely what the control freak *wants*, a given project or task is not likely to be performed correctly or to the control freak's satisfaction.

At that point, control freaks may convince themselves that they should not have delegated in the first place and that they could have in fact performed the task better if they had done it themselves. They are likely to actually take the task back from the subordinate; do it themselves; and not delegate similar tasks to these individuals again. Doing so may of course demoralize those individuals and/or inhibit their ability to grow into *their* jobs or learn to perform multiple tasks competently.

Unfortunately, what control freaks *do* sometimes tend to communicate, both by their words and by their actions, is a lack of trust in their subordinates. They can be patronizing and critical of subordinates, reminding them at every turn that they can do the job better and that the only reason they are not doing the job is that they simply do not have time.

Who Are the Nitpickers?

Nitpickers are particular types of control freaks. They get bogged down on minutia and sometimes have difficulty seeing the forest for the trees. Their particular focus, however, is on mistakes that other people make and what they perceive to be the possible negative ramifications of those mistakes.

They are the "Oh-my, the-world-is-coming-to-an-end-because-you-made-a-mistake" types. They obsess about every imperfection and call every mistake to your attention. They typically cannot distinguish between large mistakes and minor ones which will likely have no impact on the success of a given project. They sometimes have no sense that everyone makes mistakes or that not all mistakes are created equal.

They usually expect everyone, including themselves, to perform their jobs and all job tasks perfectly. They rarely provide positive reinforcement when you do perform your job perfectly because, in their minds, you simply performed as you were expected to perform and should not be excessively praised for merely "meeting expectations." They rarely miss an opportunity, however, to criticize when a mistake or imperfection occurs.

Suggested Strategies for Dealing with Control Freaks and Nitpickers

Control Freaks Generally

The following strategies apply to all control freaks, including nitpickers. (There is also a section later in the Chapter which addresses additional strategies which might be helpful in working with nitpickers in particular.)

"Go with the Flow"

One basic strategy for effectively dealing with control freaks is to just "go with the flow" and let them have their control. Try not to worry about issues over which you have no control. Try not to fight with control freaks about loosening the reins. If they want to run their business, department or staff by maintaining high levels of control, let them. You are not likely to change them anyway, at least in the short run.

If control freaks will not relinquish the necessary control to allow you to do your job effectively, there is really nothing that you can do about it until they *do* relinquish some of the control. You may need to just sit back and "let the game come to you." Control freaks will get to you when they are ready and, to some degree, the job will get done on their timetable, not yours.

If they insist upon keeping control, you may not be able to solve a given problem without their help or input. Since you do not have control over the fate of the project anyway, try to find a way not to worry about how the issue will ultimately be resolved. Try not to take it personally when these issues do not get resolved either to your satisfaction or when you would like them to.

If you have concerns (1) about a project getting done in a timely manner or correctly; (2) that a client, customer, or manager might be unsatisfied with how a project is progressing; (3) that doing a project the control freak's way would cause a substantive or strategic mistake; or (4) that doing a project the control freak's way might be detrimental to a client or to the overall project, you may need to express your concerns to the control freaks. Perhaps you can even offer suggestions for how to resolve those issues.

The control freaks will either respond by providing you with the assistance that you need or they will not. If they insist upon maintaining control and do *not* act to resolve the issue at hand in an effective manner, there is really nothing more that you can do.

If supervisor/control freaks want to maintain all contact with clients or customers, let them. If they insist on making presentations to clients, even if you believe that you can do better, let them. If they want to rewrite everything that you write and take ownership of all such items, or if they want everything that goes out under their names to reflect their styles, let them.

If they insist that they have to be involved in a particular project, let them, even if it means that you cannot proceed to the next level of what you need to do, or finish the project, without their input. Remember, it is often their neck on the line if projects are delayed or remain unfinished.

Forcing control freaks to act when they do not want to or are not ready to is likely to create the impression that they are not in control of the project or the issue. Pushing an issue with control freaks beyond what they are comfortable with is likely to make them defensive and alienate you from them, which certainly will not help you get what you want.

Give the control freaks their freedom and fight other battles on other days. Remember, it is their business/department. Let them have their control to some degree and try not to fight it unless you absolutely have to.

Control Freaks May Relinquish Some Control Over Time

If you gain the confidence and respect of control freaks, they sometimes may actually relinquish some of their control. The key is to allow them the time and space they need to gain confidence in you.

In order to gain the trust and respect of control freaks, one principal strategy is to "do the work." Do it well time and again. *Show* them that you are trustworthy and competent, and that you support them, at every opportunity. Let their confidence and trust in you and respect for you develop slowly over time. Remember to be patient, however, because that level of trust does not come easily, particularly for control freaks.

In addition, try to project confidence in your own abilities. If you show any weakness, hesitation, or lack of confidence in yourself or your abilities, control freaks will likely take over immediately and do everything themselves. Remember that they typically start out being reluctant to give *anyone* control over *anything* because, in their minds, unless proven otherwise, they can perform the tasks at hand more competently than others. Try not to give control freaks any excuse to regain control and try to give them every reason to trust *you*.

Several positive things can happen if you gain the trust and respect of control freaks. For one, because of the increased confidence that they have developed in you, you might find that you now have more credibility with them. When you *do* take a stand on a particular issue or *do* pick a particular battle, they may become more receptive to listening to what you have to say or to implementing your suggestions.

In addition, in those instances, the control freaks may actually relinquish some control. In fact, in some cases, they may even go to the other extreme and become largely uninvolved in your projects, leaving the control over all of the details to you. (You will, of course, need to decide in advance whether you are *comfortable* having that level of responsibility and control yourself.)

Communicating with Control Freaks

One key to successfully working with control freaks is to keep the lines of communication open. They like to be kept "in the loop," even if they have relinquished some level of control. Control freaks tend to become annoyed when they are led to believe, or somehow develop the impression, that they are not being kept apprised of details relating to their projects. Let them be the ones to decide what information they need to know and what they do not.

In addition, understand that, although control freaks can be very demanding, they are not necessarily unreasonable. Unlike with some of the other personality types that you might encounter at work, you often *can* reason quite productively with control freaks.

If you have a particular problem in working with control freaks, try to tactfully let them know what it is. If, for example, you believe that they need to relinquish some control in order to get a particular project done, communicate that to them as well as *why* you believe that to be the case. If you have to make the request that they take their hands off or partially off of a project, however, be delicate in your approach. Try to avoid actually using the word "control," which might be perceived to be emotionally charged or inflammatory and might be likely to make these individuals, who do not necessarily perceive themselves as "control freaks," defensive.

Inform them of *why* their actions might be impeding your ability to get things done and encourage them to give you more flexibility over the work that you personally will be performing. Couch the request in terms of *your* "additional responsibilities," rather than *their* "relinquished control." Try to limit the granting of the additional responsibilities to a particular project or for a discreet period of time because they may perceive such limited requests as being less threatening.

Do not be afraid, however, to explain why you need those additional responsibilities. Explain how the project can get done more quickly and more effectively in a given instance if they do in fact relinquish some control.

Further, sometimes you may also need to *ask* control freaks for their *assistance* in getting projects completed. In those instances, take the time to explain to them what the project will entail and the reasoning underlying your demands. Remind them of any applicable deadlines and try to explain the pressure you may be under as a result of any delay in getting the project done.

Given their propensity to want to be in control of most details anyway, you might find that they are quite receptive to assisting you in working out these problems as well.

Additional Strategies for Dealing with Nitpickers

In developing strategies for effectively responding to and working with nitpickers, you need to be aware that they tend to be perfectionists. When they point out your mistakes and perhaps even criticize you for them, they probably cannot help themselves.

Try to be sensitive to the level of pressure that the nitpickers place on themselves and understand that (1) they are probably more demanding of themselves than they are of you; (2) it is quite likely that they point out everyone's mistakes, not just yours; and (3) their nitpicking and criticisms are often not personal.

Nitpickers also are likely to be unaware that they *are* nitpicking or that the nitpicking bothers you. They commonly think that everyone focuses on the negative and on mistakes as much as they do. They think that doing so is how people manage other people and that it is simply a part of work life that everyone must endure.

Although you will obviously need to carefully pick your spots, try communicating with the nitpickers. Inform them of how their nitpicking makes you feel. Advise them of how frustrating it can sometimes be to work with them because of their emphasis on the mistakes and the negatives. Educate them on the need to provide you and others with positive reinforcement and balance, both at the particular moments of the nitpicking and generally. (To the extent that these individuals are your bosses, however, remember that you will need to be delicate and tactful, and carefully pick your spots to have these types of conversations.)

In addition, you can reduce the nitpicking and its attendant unpleasantness by making every effort to learn from your own mistakes and avoid making the same mistakes more than once. Obviously, nitpickers are less likely to nitpick if they are not confronted with the same mistakes over and over again, particularly when they have counseled others about them repeatedly.

Finally, learn to anticipate the nitpickers. Study and try to understand them; their likes; their dislikes; and what pushes their buttons. The more you learn how to avoid pushing the nitpickers' buttons, the more positive and productive your experience with the nitpickers will be.

*   *   *

In short, perhaps the best overall advice for getting along with control freaks and nitpickers at the workplace is, at least to some degree, to let them have their control and try not to take their control (or their criticism) personally. Remember, it is their business, organization, department or project. They get to run it as they see fit.

PART FIVE

Moving On

CHAPTER 15

The "Politics" of Looking for a New Job

Sometimes, despite your best efforts or for reasons beyond your control, your job cannot be salvaged and/or your work situation simply cannot be made to be more positive. When this occurs, it may be time to look for another job.

The purpose of this Chapter is to provide some suggestions for political strategies which may be useful to employ when looking for a new job. Specifically, this Chapter addresses various "human interaction" issues which may arise during a job search process, such as securing references, networking, using recruiters, and how to handle your present job responsibilities while you look for a new one.***

*** It is important to understand that an exhaustive analysis of job search and career strategies is beyond the scope of this book. For that reason, this Chapter does not cover, among other things, (1) figuring out what you want out of your job or career; (2) where to look for advertised job openings; (3) resume and cover letter preparation; (4) interviewing techniques; and (5) job negotiation strategies. For a more complete analysis of all possible job search strategies and/or a discussion of these more general

Getting References in Order

Most people should at least be aware of the *possibility* that their current jobs may not last forever and that they may need to move on at some point. You never know when the tables may turn and you find yourself in a position in which you need to look for another job. Should that happen, you should be aware that it is often difficult to get a new job without viable references, either from your existing employer or from one or more of your prior employers.

One suggestion before actually commencing a new job search is to figure out (1) *who* you want your references to be; (2) whether those individuals would be willing to *be* references for you; and (3) *what* you would like them to say. It is usually a good idea to try to line up these individuals before you actually send out letters and resumes to prospective employers. The last thing you want is to actively be pursuing another job, only to find out that you *need* a reference or that those individuals whom you thought you could count on *for* a reference are unwilling or unavailable to *be* references on your behalf.

What follows are some suggested strategies for how to secure references and maximize their interest and willingness to help you with your job search process.

Try Not to Burn Any Bridges

For many of the reasons discussed throughout this book, it is critically important to do your best at every job to avoid alienating anyone in a position of power or in a position to assist you in some capacity. You never know when you may need to call upon people from your present or past work life to help you down the line, either to provide a reference; to help you find a new job; or in some cases even to *provide* you with a new job.

---

job search strategies, you may need or desire to consult with a career counselor; attend one or more career workshops; or review any number of books whose exclusive focus is on job search and career development strategies.

Consider the following example. Margaret worked as a manager at a computer software company. She was unsatisfied with her job. She decided to explore the possibility of a career change into teaching. Although she had both personal and professional reasons for leaving, she never let on to anyone with whom she worked at the computer software company that there was anything about the job, the organization, or the people that she disliked. Rather, Margaret informed the influential persons at her company that her reasons for leaving were completely personal and that they related solely to her desire to take her career in a different direction.

For this reason, as well as the fact that she impressed all of her supervisors and managers with her work during the time that she worked there, she left the organization on very good terms. The power players in the organization were sorry to see her leave.

Once she left, Margaret also made a point of keeping in touch with many of her colleagues at her old company. She periodically politicked with several of the power players from the organization, either by speaking with them by phone or meeting with them for lunch or dinner from time to time. During these meetings, these "power players" would often make efforts at recruiting Margaret back into the fold of the organization.

Fifteen years after she left the company, her personal and professional circumstances had changed and she once again became interested in returning to her old employer. Because her relationships remained cultivated over the years, Margaret was able to pick up the phone and negotiate a mutually satisfactory deal for her return to work.

Margaret would never have been able to return to her prior employer if she had not (1) impressed the power players in that organization initially; (2) left on good terms; (3) successfully avoided alienating anyone in that organization; and (4) kept in touch.

*   *   *

As the above example illustrates, it is always a good idea to try your best to preserve the working relationships that you have developed over the years. You never know when you might need someone's help.

Securing References

Before you leave or even contemplate leaving your existing job, try to figure out who might be a good choice to provide you with a reference and is willing and able to do so. (Be aware that prospective employers sometimes insist upon speaking with people from applicants' present organizations before offering them jobs with *their* organizations.)

There is almost always *someone* with whom you have worked in *every* job who knows you well; likes you; is comfortable extolling your positive points to prospective employers; is willing to give you a reference; and whom you can trust not only to give you a positive reference, but also to have the discretion not to repeat to anyone in your present organization that you are contemplating leaving. Think about who might fit that profile.

Throughout your employment in your existing job, and particularly once you contemplate leaving, it is a good idea to put feelers out among individuals you have worked with whom you believe that you can trust. Try to convince those individuals to give you a reference. Explain, if truthful, that you may not be able to get another job without their help. Explain, if necessary, that they are in a position to help you out substantially if they would be willing to talk up your strengths for you to prospective employers. Remind them, if necessary, of what your strengths are or were.

With respect to people who might be references from your existing workplace, be careful whom you choose. Depending on the organizational relationships and/or the organizational dynamic, you may not *want* to approach, for example, the President, CEO, or other senior managers of your organization about being a reference unless you have excellent relationships with those persons and are very confident that there will be no "bad blood" between you once they are made aware that you are leaving. For these reasons, sometimes the best persons to choose for references at an existing job are likely to be mid-level managers or other persons who are not the extreme power players in your organization.

With respect to securing references from prior jobs, this process may be a bit easier in some cases than soliciting references from your existing employer. Once again, two keys to successfully preserving references from prior jobs are not to burn any bridges and to keep in touch with people after you leave. Most people, even if they are personally unwilling to work with you any longer, do not wish you any ill will and would be happy to help you succeed with your future endeavors.

Written References

Sometimes, it may even be useful to get a written reference. Some employers even *require* written letters of recommendation as part of a standard employment application.

One suggested strategy for obtaining written references is to try to make the experience as easy and as convenient for the person providing the reference as possible. For example, offer to write a draft of a letter for that person to review. Of course, such letters should highlight the positive points about you to which that individual can credibly speak and with which he or she would be willing to agree.

In addition, once the draft is approved, offer to finalize the letter by incorporating the comments or revisions made by the person providing you with the reference into it, if that is at all possible. Be aware, however, that such letters typically will need to be typed and printed on the letterhead of that person's organization before he or she can sign the letter and/or for his or her signature on such a letter to be meaningful.

Finally, whether you are involved in drafting your reference letters or your designated persons choose to draft them themselves, try to draft them in a "To-Whom-It-May-Concern" format, without being addressed to any one particular individual or organization. The purpose of doing so is so that copies can be sent to multiple prospective employers without having to continually bother these individuals to write additional letters.

Staying "Political" at Your Present Job

There are a few political strategies to keep in mind in your present job while you look for a new job. What follows is a short summary of some of the more relevant ones.

"Do the Work"

It is most important while you are looking for a new job to continue to "do the work" in your present one. Understand that it may take weeks or months (or even longer) to get another job once you commence your search.

Sometimes, people get distracted when in the midst of a job search and lose their concentration at their present job. Sometimes, once a decision to leave is made, people might mentally "check-out" of their existing jobs, perhaps long before they actually leave to start the new one.

Try your best not to lose your concentration in your present job while you look for a new job. Remember that, as long as you continue to get paid for working at your old job, you continue to have a responsibility to that organization. There is still work to be done and your old boss still has a right to expect that you will do it.

In addition, you certainly do not want to alienate anyone at your existing job, *particularly* when you are looking for a new one. The last thing that you need at that juncture is to be disciplined or, worse yet, terminated, before you are ready to make the transition to a new job. Moreover, remember that you may ultimately need some people from your existing job to provide you with references. You certainly do not want to antagonize anyone who might be in a position to help you down the road.

For all of these reasons, and as difficult as it may be, it is important that you balance the interests of your current employer against your own interests in finding a new position when embarking on your job search. Make sure you take care of yourself and do what is necessary to advance the job search efforts, but try not to "abandon ship" in the process. That will likely not serve either your short-term interests (of making your existing employment situation as positive and productive as possible while your job search process runs its course) or your long-term interests (of maximizing the likelihood of actually *getting* a new position).

Whom to Inform About Your Decision to Leave

Sometimes, you may want to discuss your interest in moving on or some details about your new job search with co-workers and supervisors at your present job. Sometimes, you have a relationship with your boss which is so close that you believe that it is appropriate to discuss these matters with him or her. Sometimes, you might feel so loyal to your present boss or your existing organization that you do not want to "leave them in the lurch" by failing to provide him or her or the organization with enough time to find a replacement for you when you leave.

In some cases, depending on the level of responsibility that you have or your relationship with your boss, it might be appropriate to give your supervisor a "heads up" about your plans. Perhaps your supervisor will even provide you with a reference and be supportive of your decision.

However, before you tell your supervisor, another manager, or even co-workers that you are looking for a new job, think long and hard about whether it is appropriate to do so and whether you are confident that you can trust those individuals. Unless you are convinced that you *can* trust those individuals, a more cautious approach might be to hold back on informing them of your plans, at least in the short run.

Understand that there are risks associated with prematurely providing your boss in particular with this kind of information. For one, your boss might believe that he or she has a responsibility to inform others in management in the organization of your status or plans. These might be individuals whom you would prefer did not know these details, at least initially.

In addition, sometimes supervisors and managers may treat you differently after you have told them of your plans to leave, even if they are outwardly supportive. You may have alienated them without realizing it. They may question your loyalty for the remaining time that you stay. They may second-guess your judgment from that point forward. They might view you as a "lame-duck" and not take you seriously or show you the respect that you deserve, whether they are aware of it or not. They might either inadvertently or intentionally give you more undesirable assignments during what they perceive to be your "lame-duck" period. They may even be resentful or envious of the fact that you are leaving.

* * *

In short, understand that every situation is different. You will need to evaluate on a case-by-case basis whom you provide with information about your job search plans and how much information to provide them. Be judicious about providing the information, however, until you trust the individuals involved and understand the potential downside risks of doing so.

Networking - Jobs through Connections and Contacts

One of the more effective ways to find a new job is through networking. Networking involves communicating with friends; family members; present work colleagues (if you can trust them); former work colleagues; former employers (with whom you have maintained positive relationships); all potential contacts that any of these individuals can refer you to; and the variety of other contacts that you have made in every conceivable life context.

The idea of networking is to spread the word among everyone you know (and hopefully among as many people as possible that *they* know) (1) that you are looking for a new job; and (2) about the type of job that you are looking for. The goal of networking is that, eventually, somewhere in the chain of contacts and connections, relevant job opportunities will present themselves to you.

It is important to note that networking can be quite advantageous for both employers and employees. From the employer's perspective, a job opening which is filled through networking is less costly because it requires less time and expense spent by the employer on recruiting. From the job seeker's perspective, getting a job through networking can be advantageous because sometimes his or her chances of actually getting an interview and/or getting the job increase dramatically when the position has not yet been advertised and there are fewer applicants for it.

*   *   *

How does one successfully network to increase his or her chances of finding a suitable new job opening? **Consider the following example.**

Annabel was a Purchasing Manager for a large company. She was looking to leave her job, but wanted to stay in the same field and in the same general locality. She was looking for a director-level position at another company because there were no openings or opportunities for advancement at her existing company.

She had worked in purchasing for nearly twenty years. She held jobs in purchasing for six different companies and had worked her way up to a manager position after working with her most recent employer for five years.

Annabel answered a variety of ads for job openings at the director level but, given the competition in the locality, did not even get an interview. She spent a considerable amount of time networking to try to find suitable job openings as well.

She had several contacts within her own company (whom she decided she *could* trust) who knew people in her industry and at competitor companies. Although none of those contacts actually knew of any job openings themselves, each gave her one or two names of people who might know of openings. In addition, she also contacted people whom she herself knew in her industry and/or in her particular specialty or whom she had heard of as working in her industry or specialty.

Annabel left no stone unturned in her networking process. She contacted everyone she could think of who could conceivably help her. She followed up with these individuals every few months. She also contacted every individual to whom her own contacts had referred her.

In addition, at social occasions with family or friends, she continued to make a point of mentioning that she was looking for a new job. She would take opportunities whenever they presented themselves on such occasions to describe her field and the type of position she was looking for. She would commonly ask those individuals to keep their eyes and ears open for her. Occasionally, she would even obtain the names of some people to contact from those individuals. She would then of course contact all of those new individuals as well. She also contacted individuals from her high school and college days whom she thought might be able to help her.

Over a period of six to eight months, Annabel developed a strong support network of acquaintances and colleagues. Through this process, she eventually came across a few people who actually had job openings in their organizations or had actually heard of openings elsewhere. Once informed of the openings, Annabel contacted the employers directly to try to find out more about the positions; sell herself as a potential candidate for the positions if appropriate; and schedule interviews with those employers whenever possible.

Nine months after commencing her job search, and after

extensive networking, Annabel hit "paydirt." One of the contacts that she made through networking was looking for a director-level person in purchasing. The position had not yet been advertised. The employer was immediately impressed with Annabel's credentials. The chain of contacts that led Annabel to the employer was quite credible.

After an initial meeting with Annabel and her having several follow-up interviews with other members of senior management, one of the principals at this new organization offered Annabel the job. She accepted the position, which, as it turned out, played to her strengths. She has remained extremely happy in that position ever since.

*   *   *

As the above example illustrates, individuals can find the positions that they are looking for through persistent networking. In addition, the Annabel scenario teaches us a number of things about how to network successfully for a new job. What follows is a summary of some of the more salient points in that regard.

On its most basic level, successful networking involves keeping your antennae up; having friends, colleagues and contacts do the same; being opportunistic; recognizing realistic opportunities when they present themselves; and jumping on them when they *do* come up.

In addition, be aware that networking requires that individuals not be shy about talking to contacts from whatever source about potential employment opportunities. Networking requires an understanding that individuals whom you know or with whom you speak directly (at least initially) may not themselves know of any job opportunities that are suitable for you. Networking requires you to encourage your own direct contacts to keep you in mind if they *do* hear about either job openings or other contacts that might be useful for you to make.

Further, it is important to understand that networking can sometimes be a less direct and a more time-consuming job search process than merely responding to an ad for a job opening can be. Successful job search networking takes time; requires patience; and takes perseverance.

Finally, it is also important to understand that answering ads for job openings and job search networking are not mutually exclusive. In order to maximize your search efforts, you can and should explore all possible openings from every source, including from networking and advertised openings.

Using Recruiters to Assist in Your Job Search

Recruiters are agencies or individuals hired by some employers to find suitable candidates for their job openings. They solicit resumes and/or applications on behalf of the employers and initially screen applicants for those employers. It is not uncommon for employers who hire recruitment firms to delay in separately advertising their particular job openings or forego advertising altogether. Rather, employers who use recruiters commonly rely on them to present a small pool of qualified candidates for open positions. In those situations, the only way to even discover those openings is to contact recruiters and ascertain what openings they might have in their particular databases.

Recruiters can be extremely helpful to individuals who are searching for a new job. They typically work for a number of employers and commonly have access to any number of listings. In addition, employers who hire recruiters often trust their judgment to provide them with viable candidates. For that reason, getting an introduction to an employer with a job opening through a recruiter might in some cases even be more advantageous than attempting to contact an employer directly. In short, the recruiter may provide you with a way to get your foot in the door with an employer that you might not have been able to get without the recruiter's help.

Recruitment firms commonly assist professional people or

people working in office-type jobs. In addition, recruitment firms usually are highly specialized in that they often place individuals only in a certain field. Because of these specialties, it is important that you figure out which type of recruiter specializes in placing people in your field with your particular skill set in your particular locality, so that you can find the right recruiter to work with in finding you suitable employment.

*   *   *

The keys to successfully working with recruiters is to pick the right one for your needs and to develop an understanding of their agendas and/or what motivates *them* to work hard to try to place *you*. **Consider the following example.**

Mark was a department manager at a small, privately-held company in Portland, Oregon. He worked at that facility for ten years. He reached a point at which he believed that he had gone as far as he could with that job. He wanted to work for a larger company, perhaps in a larger market.

Mark commenced a nationwide job search for such a position and contacted a recruitment agency to assist him in his search. He and his family were willing to relocate anywhere for the right opportunity.

Kate, a principal at the recruitment agency that Mark contacted, indicated that there was a company located in New York City which had an opening for which Mark might be suitable. She explained that she believed that the salary was at the low end of the range that Mark had determined would be acceptable, particularly if a cross-country move would be involved. She also informed Mark that, in her experience with New York companies of this size that were hiring at this level, and given that there were so many applicants from the New York environs from which employers could choose, this particular company would not, in all likelihood, be willing to pay either for Mark to fly to New York for an interview or for moving expenses if he was offered and accepted the position.

Based on those initial representations, Mark was reluctant to pursue the opportunity at all. In a subsequent phone call, however, Kate indicated to Mark that she thought that there would be "room to negotiate" with respect to the initial salary number that she had given him and that the New York company might be willing to provide additional perks and benefits for the right candidate.

At that point, Mark decided to at least find out more information about the job from the employer directly. He asked Kate to forward his materials to the New York company. He indicated to Kate, however, that, given his own time commitments, he would only travel to New York at his own expense if this company was seriously interested in him; and, even then, if it would consider paying him a salary which was $20,000 higher than what she initially informed him that the job was likely to pay. He indicated to Kate that it would not be worth his and his family's while to pursue an opportunity in New York unless the prospective employer was willing to spend that kind of money. He also figured in the back of his mind that, if this company was that serious about him, reimbursement for moving expenses would be negotiable directly with the prospective employer.

Kate assured Mark at that point that the company was "extremely interested" in him and that, although she had no authority to communicate a specific dollar figure to Mark, she was "confident" that the salary issue could be worked out in a range that he would find acceptable. (She led him to believe that she had "inside" information which supported that representation.) She also indicated, however, that, if Mark were seriously interested, he needed to get on a plane to New York right away, because the company was looking to fill the position immediately.

Based upon those representations, Mark flew to New York at his own expense to meet with the principal decision-makers at the New York company. Although he interviewed with several high-level people, it became evident during these discussions that (1) the company was under the impression that Mark was in

New York on other business anyway and did not make a special trip just to interview there; (2) the company had not even determined whether there was in fact going to be an opening for the position he sought; (3) the company was not "seriously" interested in him, as became evident by the fact that several of the principals were looking at his materials for the first time in his presence during the interview meetings; (4) the principals who had reviewed his materials were merely "curious" about him before he came to New York and informed the recruiter that, if Mark was going to be in New York anyway, he should stop by to meet some people; and (5) if an opening for the position was going to arise, the salary for the position would be in the low end of the range that Mark had discussed with Kate, not at the high end.

Certainly, Mark would not have made the trip to New York had Kate correctly informed him about the company's true state of mind with respect to this opening. In addition, as it turned out, the New York company decided not to even create an opening for the position that Mark sought.

Given this experience, Mark became disillusioned about using Kate or other recruiters to help him with his job search. He expressed his dissatisfaction and concern to Kate about how he believed that she had misled him.

However, Mark was also keenly aware that Kate had numerous contacts throughout the country which Mark could not cultivate himself in his job search. He realized that Kate could open doors for him that he could not possibly open for himself. He understood that it was still important and potentially beneficial for him to continue to ask her for assistance in finding suitable job openings for him, assuming that he could figure out a way to maintain a positive and productive working relationship with her.

Based on this experience, Mark decided that the best way to make his relationship with Kate work to his advantage was to better communicate exactly what he wanted to her; insist that he would not continue to work with her unless she was completely direct and honest with him and respected his preferences; and keep as much control over the job interview and negotiation processes as he possibly could. He began to view Kate and recruiters generally as individuals whose principal function was to make the initial contacts with employers.

Kate realized that Mark was an attractive candidate for companies throughout the country. She understood that, if Mark was ultimately hired through her contacts, she would get a commission. Kate understood that it was not in her best interests to alienate Mark, any more than it was in his best interests to alienate her.

Mark eventually found a job in Chicago through Kate's initial introduction. Mark negotiated for his own salary and perks and was reimbursed for all travel and moving expenses, while Kate received her commission.

*　　*　　*

The Mark/Kate example illustrates some problems that can develop in dealing with recruiters, as well as some ways to effectively work *with* them. What follows is a summary of some basic points to keep in mind and understand about recruiters and working with them, as well as some suggested strategies to employ to maximize the advantages of using recruiters to assist you in your job search.

Recruiters Work on Commission

Individuals who use recruiters need to understand that their business is sales. Their agendas are to place people in jobs and make commissions from employers for those placements. Be aware that their goal is to close deals in exchange for their fees.

That is not to say that they will not work hard to try to make placements. Certainly the better recruiters will look to find candidates that fit well with the particular organizations they work with. Their incentive for doing so, however, is that they receive a commission (usually from the employer) for each placement they make.

Recruiters Are Not Your Agents

Be aware that, although recruiters work with individuals to try to place them, for the most part, they are not the "agents" of those individuals. Recruiters essentially work for the employers. They get paid by the employers. Their job is to make connections between employers and prospective employees.

True "agents," like those who represent actors, artists, and writers, for example, are frequently authorized to *negotiate* on behalf of the "individual" clients whom they represent; often handle various types of business affairs for their clients; and typically have long-standing, ongoing relationships *with* their "individual" clients. Those agents might be paid by their "individual" clients directly or may be paid a commission for each transaction that they successfully negotiate for their "individual" clients. They are often hired for the specific purpose of making deals on behalf of their "individual" clients and it is their "individual" clients who pay them, in one form or another, for their services.

By contrast, recruiters' longstanding relationships are typically with employers. They are less akin to a true "agent," who "represents" an "individual," and more akin to a "matchmaker" who, in exchange for a fee, brings two parties together to create a deal that they can both live with. Although some employers and employment candidates choose to allow recruiters to act as a "go-betweens" in negotiations, often times recruiters' roles are simply to get the parties together and not actually negotiate the deal for them at all.

Everyone Benefits from a Recruiter's Placement

It is ultimately in everyone's best interests for a recruiter to find suitable candidates who are a good fit for their employer clients. The candidates will ultimately be happy. In addition, should they ever desire to move again at some point for any reason, they will be likely to use that recruiter again if their overall experience was positive. Those individuals also will be more likely to recommend the recruiter to their friends, colleagues, and other contacts if the placement experience was positive.

Further, and perhaps more importantly from the recruiters' perspective, if they succeed in placing suitable candidates with a particular organization, the *organization* is likely to use them again. Organizations have a variety of job openings which arise from time to time. The easier and more successful the experience with the recruiter has been, the more likely the organization will use that recruiter again for other placements.

In short, although recruiters work on commission and are paid by employers, successful placements and positive placement experiences can create a "win" situation for everyone involved.

Keep as Much Control as Possible

As an individual looking for a job and using a recruiter, try to keep as much control over the situation as possible. Be aware, however, that recruiters have different styles and have different kinds of relationships with different kinds of employers. As is noted earlier in this Chapter, some employers hire recruiters to handle all negotiations between the organization and the applicant. Some employers simply use the recruiter to make the connections. Some employers might speak to the applicant through the recruiter, who acts as a liaison between the two and conveys all offers and counter-offers without actually doing any of the negotiating.

Depending upon the applicant's qualifications and experience level, it can be in the applicant's overall best interests, however, to keep as much control over the process as possible. Try to view the recruiter's job in your case as one of merely making the initial introduction, if you possibly can. Unless the employer insists on dealing only with the recruiter, you should play an active part in every step of the interview and negotiating process.

Communicate clearly with the recruiter about exactly what it is that you want; what is acceptable to you; and what is not acceptable to you. Try to put yourself in a position in which *you* are in control of communications and/or the setting up of all meetings after the initial meeting, if that is at all possible.

Speak for yourself and negotiate for yourself, if possible. In many cases, you can articulate your strengths, interests and needs better than the recruiter can on your behalf, particularly if you do not have an ongoing or longstanding relationship with the recruiter. The recruiter can certainly give you pointers about strategies regarding what to say to employers and/or how to negotiate with them (since they usually *do* have longstanding and ongoing relationships with those employers), but, whenever possible, try not to let recruiters speak or negotiate on your behalf to any extent greater than you believe is necessary under the circumstances of your particular situation.

In addition, with respect to negotiation, although you can use the recruiter as a guide, do not necessarily take the recruiter's word that certain things are not attainable. If there are certain things that you believe you "must have" in order to close the deal, and those things are reasonable and not too far-reaching by market standards, you may want to try to negotiate for them despite the recruiter's advice to the contrary. (A perfect example of that is Mark's success in the previous example in negotiating for travel and moving expenses to be reimbursed by his future employer.)

Remember, this is *your* job; *your* family; *your* future. The recruiters' stakes in the outcome of their placements are that they stand to make a commission if the placement is successful. Only *you* can to decide whether this opportunity is right for you. One important way to do that is to be as proactive as you possibly can be at every step of the interview and negotiation process.

Before You Start

In order to do your best work and make the best first impression that you can at your new job, you want to be as relaxed as possible, given the other circumstances in your life at the time, *before* you start working. In order to accomplish this, it is usually helpful to think ahead and anticipate exactly what you will need to accomplish and how much time you will need to accomplish it *before* you start working.

If you need some time to attend to some personal, professional or other work-related matters before you start, try to discuss those issues with your new employer either during the negotiation stage of the process or, at a minimum, in advance of your anticipated start date. If you have to move, try to factor that in. If you are already stressed out from your existing job or the "wrap-up" process from your existing job, and you need some time off simply to relax before starting your new job, factor that in as well. If you have a preplanned vacation, let your future employer know that and try to arrange to start afterwards if possible.

Do not be afraid to discuss these issues with your new employer. Although employers usually are in a hurry to fill a position and complete their interviewing and decision-making process, many *are* willing to accommodate things like timing and start dates for the right candidate.

Remind your future employer if necessary and appropriate that hopefully you and the employer will be together for a long time. Try to explain that the difference of a few weeks here or there in order to start a new job without unnecessary, extraneous stresses really should not make that much of a difference in the life of your entire projected employment with the organization. Explain that it would be useful and necessary for you to take the time now so that you can truly "hit the ground running" when you actually commence working for the organization. It certainly makes sense to put your best foot forward and start a job when you are truly ready to "dig in," rather than to start working before you are ready for whatever reason.

*　　*　　*

In short, try not to put unnecessary pressure on yourself *before* you start working at a new job, so that you can maximize your chances for making your experience at your new job as positive, productive and pleasant as it possibly can be.

INDEX